MW00564646

SHENANDOAH VOICES

Folklore, Legends and

Traditions of the Valley

John L. Heatwole

November 16, 1996

To Dacha,
The curse I had hoped
would not happen; the young
lady's name was Dascha.

John Heatwole

Rockbridge Publishing Company
Berryville, Virginia

Published by

Rockbridge Publishing Company
P.O. Box 351
Berryville, VA 22611
(703) 955-3980

Photographs courtesy of: Minnie Carr (p. 5); Carroll Dennison (p. 79); Arbutus Godfrey (p. 53); Paul H. Heatwole (p. 125); Cheryl Lyon (p. 105); Lula Mae Miller (p. 55); Jean and Bill O'Brien (p. 96); Patricia T. Ritchie (p. 69); Ken Schuler (drawing: dustjacket and p. 70); Vinton Southard (p.10); and Francis Wayland (pp. 109, 116). All other photographs are from the author's collection.

Library of Congress Cataloging-in-Publication Data

Heatwole, John. 1948–
    Shenandoah voices : folklore, legends, and traditions of the
Valley / John Heatwole. — 1st ed.
        p.   cm.
    Includes bibliographical references and index.
    ISBN 1-883522-07-2
    1. Folklore—Shenandoah River Valley (Va. and W. Va.)
    2. Shenandoah River Valley (Va. and W. Va.)—Social life and
customs.   I. Title.
    GR108.H43   1995
    398'.09755'9—dc20   95-8763
                                                        CIP

10   9   8   7   6   5   4   3   2

For Miriam and David ... my own ones
and
Uncle Paul ... your message came through

Contents

Foreword

In this book, John Heatwole attempts to bring to life the folklore of a place that he deeply loves—Virginia's Shenandoah Valley. Unfortunately, in today's modern world of science, technology and rapid communications, the place and importance of folklore in our lives has come to be badly misunderstood and discounted. Ironically, at a time when information and knowledge are considered to be the essence of success and human well-being, earlier ways of acquiring and transmitting such understanding are being assigned to the realm of curiosity and ignorant simplicity. Folklore is timeless, and is as much a product of modern peoples who are trying to find their way within societies that are becoming increasingly more complex and personally demanding, as it was to the generations who passed before.

Folklore is fragile in that the vehicle of its communication is often verbal, taking the form of stories, philosophies, songs, or information passed by word of mouth. In many instances, standards of community illiteracy contributed to the circumstance. In other cases, its documentation simply was not seen as necessary, much of the information being treated as "common knowledge" or "common sense."

Often spoken, occasionally written, folklore is the beliefs, values, and knowledge that address very real and basic daily needs of individuals coping with a frequently hostile or at least challenging world. Bigger than life characters, who may or may not have existed, are often used as role models whose skills and abilities are to be emulated. Moralistic stories set standards of behavior which often explain the merit of expected behavior and justify punishments for those who fail to accept those ways of living. In many instances, the events portrayed reveal a folk history designed to reinforce and explain current values or customs. The perceived realities of magic, witchcraft, ghosts and evil powers provide understanding for people seeking to explain personal disaster. Statements pertaining to planting, curing, cooking, etc., that today are overlooked, in their time and place were practical statements of experience which served to aid in making important decisions about very real issues of daily life. In other cases, the telling of stories, regardless of their content, was one way of passing a pleasant and entertaining evening.

Perhaps in our era of computerized logic, space exploration, laser surgery, and agri-business, we have outgrown the need for "folklore." Instead of recognizing it for the critical role it played, and continues to play, we choose to deny its relevance. Witches, ghosts, and goblins are too infantile to people who "know it all." Potions and charms are of little meaning to people who go to pharmacies; and the ramblings of farm almanacs hold little value to students of scientific climatology.

It is too bad. While we might debate the need and place of folklore in our modern society, to students of social history, the folklore of past eras represents one portrayal of the realities of those times as they were seen and given meaning by the people who lived them. While many of these early beliefs are now proven incorrect, they were, at that time, some of the best explanations available to people having to confront often stressful situations without the benefit of more modern knowledge or technology.

Unfortunately, in our race into the twentieth and now twenty-first century, many of us have chosen to leave the old ways behind. In a recent project, I had the opportunity to research the folklore and folk history of a section of Bath and Highland counties in Virginia. In talking with informants, many of whom were in their 70s, they routinely commented about how their children and the youth of the day just weren't interested in hearing about the old times and the old ways. For these people, the knowledge they held, valued, and had lived much of their lives by, simply wasn't being passed down or even recognized as important. As each member of the community died, more and more of the "common knowledge" was being lost and it just seemed that nobody cared anymore. These informants were enthusiastic contributors; first because it allowed them the opportunity to recall the old times that were their lives, but also because to them these bits of information were important and still held meaning.

In John Heatwole, the ghosts that haunt the hills and hollows of the Valley, the community of witches and curers, the Gypsy Queen, and just plain folk, like Ben Southard, have found a friend; and in his book they have found a new voice. I have known John for more than fifteen years, during which I have spent many an hour listening to him recant old stories and excitedly tell me of a "new one he just heard." John is a romantic, and in many ways a person who is out of his time. Nevertheless, he is a very serious scholar, and a true student of Valley history. While he is a story teller of the old school, and can throw out yarns with the best of them, when he hears new stories or philosophies, he seeks to know their origin, validate their authenticity, and understand their meanings. As someone who loves the Valley and comes from a family that has significantly contributed to its heritage, John has been most successful in turning his sensitivity to its culture into a very distinctive physical art. Now he is trying something else.

Clarence R. Geier
Professor of Anthropology
James Madison University
Harrisonburg, Virginia

Acknowledgments

The research for this book spans two decades. During that time I've spoken to hundreds of people about my interest in the folklore of the Shenandoah Valley. I am sure that there are individuals who have contributed to this work whose names I have forgotten or overlooked in preparing these acknowledgments; any oversight was not intentional and hopefully will be forgiven.

Julie Swope acted as a preliminary editor as she waded through a profusion of handwritten pages while typing the manuscript. Her observations and suggestions have been invaluable. Julie's mother, Elizabeth Fitzwater, read each chapter and caught some errors before they became engraved in stone. Jim Swope carried material and messages back and forth and accompanied me on several excursions into the hinterland to gather information. Kathie Tennery of Rockbridge Publishing responded to the idea for this book early on and stayed with it.

Randall Stover listened for years and kept the idea alive to bring the tales together in this form.

The Rockingham County Board of Supervisors gave permission to use excerpts from tapes made during the county's bicentennial in the period from 1975 through 1978. Lorraine La Prevotte conducted many of the bicentennial interviews with great care and grace.

Nelson Alexander of the Shenandoah Valley Civil War Roundtable introduced me to several informants and accompanied me on the interviews. Ruth Greenawalt and her staff at the Alexander Mack Memorial Library of Bridgewater College hunted up specific references and made me aware of sources with which I had been unfamiliar. The late Grace Showalter of the Menno Simons Library of Eastern Mennonite

College helped me with information about the early Mennonite settlers of the Valley.

All of the staff of the Rockingham County Public Library and Genealogical Research Room have been generous for years with their help and encouragement. The staff of the Carrier Library and Special Collections of James Madison University on several occasions verified particular accounts. Faye Witters and her staff at the Harrisonburg–Rockingham Historical Society Library in Dayton were always very helpful when called upon.

My thanks to the staffs of the Augusta County Public Library in Fishersville, the Staunton Public Library, and the Handley Library in Winchester for their help while using their collections. Dick and Ellen Swanson gave support in so many ways.

Dr. M. Ellsworth Kyger of Bridgewater shared several family tales, and he translated some of the Pennsylvania German documents. Sue Eckstein, of Rockville, Maryland, also did translations and suggested how this particular material could be presented. Matt Salo of The Gypsy Lore Society provided invaluable information.

Dr. Clarence Geier offered valuable observations during our many conversations about the social history of the Valley. Patricia Turner Ritchie clarified information concerning people in the Brocks Gap area of Rockingham County. Mensel Dean put me on the track of an unusual Civil War story, and Linda Dean introduced me to the Roman area of Augusta County. I am also grateful to Lawrence D. Bowers, Jr., for making me aware of the George Edgar Sipe Papers, and Dr. George Hedrick for kindly giving permission to quote from them.

Marilyn M. Dale, my mother-in-law, gave me encouragement and a beautiful setting in Myrtle Beach, South Carolina, overlooking the Atlantic Ocean, where I wrote the chapter on Valley witches and witch doctors. My sister and brother-in-law, Stephanie and George Price, cheered me on with their interest during the long months. My wife Miriam and son David have, as always, been my most honest critics and most loving supporters.

Finally, to all of those people who have shared their memories and stories, and especially the late Paul V. Heatwole, this book is more yours than mine.

J. L. H.
Bridgewater, Virginia
in the Shenandoah Valley

Introduction

Folktales usually fall into one of three categories: humorous, ironic or profound. They have evolved in every age and culture. Because they are out of the ordinary or at least slightly skewed from what most people think of as normal, they are memorable.

Sometimes folklore is perceived as a body of stories made up out of whole cloth, and some of the most famous ones are. Consider Paul Bunyan and his blue ox, Babe, and the wild and wooly Pecos Bill. These, I would submit, are New World fairy tales and should not be classified as folklore. For me, folktales have always risen from the lives of real people, and although they are often about fantastic happenings or super human deeds, somewhere back in time there was a kernel of truth that sparked the telling. These stories take us to a time when the pace of life was governed by the seasons and the every-day needs of the community. They should be cherished and preserved, because they are the color commentary to straight history. Before the advent of radio and television, conversation was the main source of communication—and in some remote areas it was the only way the people were connected with the rest of mankind.

The beautiful Shenandoah Valley of Virginia is fertile and healthy ground for the growth and sustenance of folktales. Because of the barrier of the Blue Ridge Mountains, the early settlers were cut off from the rest of the Commonwealth both physically and psychologically. They came into a land with vast, dark virgin forests, brooding hills and hollows and broad, grassy plains. The dangers they faced in the new land were sometimes secondary to the loneliness of life in the wilds.

Most of them were born in northern Europe or in the British Isles, or were only a few generations removed from the hearty folk who had crossed "the pond" to America. When they filtered into the Valley from Pennsylvania and Maryland, they brought with them age-old traditions and superstitions. While the German-Swiss and those of German-Swiss ancestry were considered to be greatly influenced by folk beliefs and superstitions, the Scots-Irish were not far behind. In the passage of 250 years, traditions in the two communities have become mixed to some extent, especially in the category of folk remedies.

The belief in witches was common in all of the Valley counties, but there is no record of a suspected witch being jailed or killed. It seemed enough to identify them and counter their spells with the good magic of a witch doctor. Witch doctors were called in more often than medical doctors when strange illnesses arose, and they were believed to have the ability to nullify hexes on livestock, buildings and personal property.

It was said that a witch doctor could not pass on his or her power to a member of the same sex or a near relative or the power would be diminished. Incantations used by witch doctors to counteract hexes were highly guarded. We know of some of them through rare publications, mostly in German, which detail the methodology of white magic. They are sometimes called "Pow Wow Books."

Tall tales abound in the Shenandoah Valley. They include ghost stories, amazing feats of strength and tales of subtle irony. They are formed from extraordinary events in the everyday lives of real people.

One evening I went with my friend Randy Stover to visit a woman who lived in the shadow of the Alleghenies. She and Randy are distantly related and have ancestors in common. We sat at her kitchen table, where she had laid out old newspaper clippings and photographs for us.

When I interview a subject, I ask questions that I hope will lead the person to memories of long-forgotten people and events. I asked the kind lady if she remembered any superstitions or supernatural happenings. She paused for a moment, as if she were trying to recall something that might be of interest to me, then stammered, "I don't think I do." Just then Randy, looking at a photograph, interrupted with, "Isn't this my great-grandfather?" To my disappointment, I thought he had totally diverted her attention from my question.

She spoke with Randy for just a few seconds, confirming the identify of the man in the photograph, then suddenly and smoothly she turned back to me and said, "Well, there was this witch—"

While there are new folk stories being born every day, the people who have ties with the 19th century are rapidly fading away.

Listen ... and you will hear their voices.

Valley Folk

All it takes for a story to become folklore is for someone in a community to do something out of the ordinary and for someone else in the community to tell a third person. The majority of the stories that are passed along involve local characters and eccentrics, the folks who prompt us to stop our friends on the street or at the farm bureau and ask, "Did you hear what so-and-so did yesterday?" Thus begins the telling. And the listeners are all ears, because the subject of the tale is usually known far and wide for a peculiar, even perverse, sense of humor, or for causing or becoming involved in fantastic situations. With luck the tale will become a favorite and will be passed on down through the years.

Other people become the subject of a story because of a single defining moment in their lives. These stories are usually touched with irony and lead us to quiet reflection.

For every tale in this chapter, no matter how small, there are thousands that have been lost. They were the pulse of a bygone era that gave it a richness, texture and color.

The Master is Not at Home

Near Leetown in Jefferson County is the limestone house called Prato Rio, purchased in 1775 by a former British officer named Charles Lee. At the outbreak of the American Revolution, Lee threw his lot in with the Colonists. He resented that Congress had named George Washington to command the fledgling army, feeling that his experience warranted his own appointment to the position. As it was, he was made second-in-command.

When Lee bungled the initial American assault at the battle of Monmouth Court House in New Jersey in 1778, Washington roared onto the field hurling furious oaths and relieved Lee of command. The commanding general then stemmed the tide of retreating men and fought the British to a standstill.

The result of this, and his involvement in a plot against Washington in a secret conspiracy, was Lee's suspension from the army. He returned to his estate with his Italian bodyguard, his slaves and his hunting dogs and went into seclusion.

Lee was known to be an eccentric of the highest order. The first floor of his house was without partitions. He marked it off with chalk into four quarters; in one was his bed, in another his kitchen equipment, his books were in another section and the fourth contained his saddles and guns.

A few years after the war, Washington was in the area visiting relatives, and he decided to pay a visit to Lee. He sent a note saying he would stop by the next day and hoped that they "could meet as old friends and comrades-in-arms," leaving their former contentions in the past.

When General Washington arrived at Prato Rio the next day, he found the house locked and, to all appearances, deserted. Tacked to the front door was a simple note: "No meat cook'd here today." Charles Lee had obviously not sent his respects to his old commander.[1]

The Lonely Spot

The widower John Allen was considered quite a catch in early 19th century Augusta County. Not only was he a member of one of the most well established and prosperous families in this section of the Valley, he had boundless energy and showed great promise of becoming a success in his own right. There weren't many enterprises around the town of Staunton that he didn't explore for opportunities to enrich himself.

Perhaps in the young widow Ann McCue he saw a way to strengthen his financial situation; marrying to increase one's holdings was an acceptable part of business in his day. In any event, they married, and there are indications that John and Ann soon developed a bond of affection for one another. They had children, and Ann kept house and tried to make life comfortable for John as he speculated on various business schemes and land ventures.

By the time the children were almost grown, John's convoluted fund raising practices had brought them to the brink of ruin. Investors and creditors were no longer willing to forgive or overlook John Allen's extensive unpaid debts. He was unable to raise sufficient funds to meet his obligations, so he fled his responsibilities, heading for the Northwest Territory, where men with energy could make a new start in life. His ignominious flight was seen as even more odious because he left Ann behind to endure the whispers and sidelong glances of their neighbors.

Gravestone of Ann Allen in the Augusta Stone Church Cemetery, Fort Defiance, Virginia.

Some people say he was gone for as long as two years before he sent word to Ann to join him, but when word came, she did not hesitate. She made her way to her husband's side in the wilds of the territory of Michigan, where she found that he had gotten back on his feet and seemed to be rebuilding his reputation as well as his fortune. Most important of all to her, though, was the fact that he had sent for her.

John had established a town, and he was involved in supplying lot holders with the materials necessary to erect business structures and dwellings. For a time all went well for the Allens, and on the surface John seemed to have learned a lesson from his earlier experience. The town was a success, and new settlers arrived almost daily. But then, as before, it became apparent that John Allen was dangerously over-extended. With no other recourse, his creditors had to finally put the law on him. Once again, as he had in Virginia, he fled westward, leaving Ann behind. But this time it was for good—John Allen disappeared and was never heard from again.

Ann eventually returned to Augusta County, where she lived with her son's family for the rest of her life. She died in 1875 and was laid to rest in the cemetery of Augusta Stone Church at Fort Defiance, Virginia. If you enter the burial ground from the south and go about halfway down the path, you will see two tall stone obelisks on the left. Just about opposite the second one, on the right side of the path, there is a small white stone that marks Ann Allen's grave. It is a simple monument to a woman whose only lasting gift from her husband was that he had named a town for her in the forests of Michigan—Ann's Arbor, now Ann Arbor, Michigan.[2]

The Great Bully of the Hills of Judea

Robert Misner was born in the mid-1820's at the village of Roman in Augusta County. His father was the blacksmith there, and Robert, following in his footsteps, also became a blacksmith.

Robert Misner, the Great Bully of
the Hills of Judea

Big Robert Misner was known for his prowess as a brawler. Fighting in that era was something of a pastime, and the great fighters, horse racers, hunters, wrestlers, marksmen and fishermen were the sports heros of the day. For many years Robert was at the top of his sport. His fame as "Fighting Bob" Misner and "the Great Bully of the Hills of Judea" was known far and wide.[3]

When the Civil War began, Fighting Bob immediately enlisted in the 10th Virginia Cavalry. He served throughout the four years of the conflict, even though he could have avoided service because of his age.[4]

While he was in the service, he heard rumors of a new "Great Bully" in the Hills, and the reports were confirmed when he returned home after the war. It was more than he could stand, so he rolled up his sleeves and went to the home of his rival for a confrontation.

He found a young man, built as powerfully as himself, and it was obvious that he had been expecting the visit. There were no formalities; the two men got right down to the business of trying to destroy one another.

The fight was a long, drawn out one. It could have been called even for a while, but Bob's age began to tell and his legendary endurance began to slacken. Soon he was taking more than he was giving. Finally he was down, unable to answer the call to stand. He knew the end had come, but he summoned up enough strength to struggle to his feet one last time. He took the young man's hand in his and shook it as he proclaimed "the new Champion of the Hills."[5]

Fighting Bob moved out of the heart of the Hills over a little way to the village of Milne (present day Centerville), near the Rockingham County line, where he took up his blacksmith's trade again, raised a family and lived peaceably with his neighbors.

Fighting Bob Misner rests in the St. Michael's Church Cemetery. His grave is unmarked.[6]

Bill Flemings

Bill Flemings, who lived across Dry River from the village of Rushville, was a dyed-in-the-wool, 110-per-cent certified character. He was born in 1859 and lived until the middle of the 20th century. Mostly he was an itinerant farm worker, having labored at one time or another on almost every farm in southwestern Rockingham County. He thought of himself as a witch doctor, but his opinion of himself as a being with superior powers to remove spells and hexes and to confuse the designs of witches was not shared by the community at large. Most folks grudgingly recognized him only as a fairly effective wart doctor.

Bill Flemings (1859-1946)
Wart doctor and extraordinary farmhand

Once, when he was a young man, he and his friend Jake Clayton decided to try their luck as highwaymen. They set out to waylay a wealthy stockman as he returned one evening from a cattle sale in Harrisonburg, the county seat. They planned to spring upon their target as he rode along a lonely path through the woods. Bill was to pull the horse up by the bit while Jake dragged the man from the saddle. The plan was simple enough, but as Bill tried to grab the horse, the stockman kicked out with his right foot and destroyed one of Bill's eyes. With his riding crop he drove Jake back into the brush.[7] This ended Bill's career as an outlaw, and ever after he said he lost his eye to an illness.

There are many stories about Bill robbing hen and smoke houses. In most of these tales, the ill-gotten goods are either retrieved or returned.

You might wonder why such an untrustworthy fellow would be tolerated, but the fact was that he had talents of real value to his neighbors. His strength and endurance as a farm laborer were legendary.

Non-believers who put him to the test were usually astonished at the outcome. One day Bill was walking by Muddy Creek Mill when Mr. Simmers, the mill operator, called out to him to come over. As usual, there were quite a few men around—mill hands, farmers and assorted loungers.

Mr. Simmers threw out a challenge. "Bill, we'll give you a barrel of flour if you can carry it on your shoulder to your house without putting it down 'til you get there." This was a daunting proposal, at least to most of the men watching, for a barrel of flour weighed in at 196 pounds.

Bill didn't blink. "How 'bout the bran and the shorts for my hogs?"he asked. That would add another 36 pounds to the load.

The miller agreed, and the barrel was hoisted to Bill's shoulder from the dock, the sack of offal laid on top. A mill hand was sent along to verify the outcome. The journey was more than a mile and partly uphill. The last leg crossed the Dry River bridge—his home was just on the other side. When he got to his back door, Bill didn't even ask his young escort to help him off-load the burden. With a mighty heave, he plunked it down in the dust, thus meeting another challenge.[8]

Another time, while working on the Shank farm threshing wheat, Bill decided to show off for the farmer's young sons, Glenn and Wade. The wheat had been bagged at two sixty-pound bushels to the bag. Bill had the boys tie his hands behind his back, then he leaned over and picked up the 120-pound bag with his teeth. He swung it slowly back and forth until the rhythm was just right, and then, with a mighty jerk of his head, he straightened his back and slung the sack onto his right shoulder.[9]

Some years later, when the Shank boys were teenagers, they were out in a field cutting cornstalks and building shocks when Bill came ambling by. After watching for a minute or two, he asked, "Need any help, Glenn?" The boys called for him to"come on over." They couldn't keep up with the old man as he built two shocks for each of theirs.[10]

One of Bill's best friends was Hiram Whitmer. Hiram walked the countryside doing odd jobs mostly, and at harvest time he and Bill hired out as a team to the local farmers. They cut corn, reaped grains, baled hay, threshed wheat and filled silos, cribs and barns. They made a game out of the work, each trying to outdo the other. It was a sight to see the two men swinging huge grain cradles and moving through a vast bottomland field of wheat like machines.[11]

Bill knew how to relax, too. One fellow who was a boy in the 1940s remembered seeing him sitting in the sun on his pink sandstone front step playing his fiddle.[12] Bill's face was pinched and puckered on the side where the eye was missing. A child, doing as children sometimes do, asked Bill why his face looked so funny. Bill replied that his face was that way because when he was a baby the sun shone through the handle-hole of his cradle, and he squinted so much that his face drew up permanently on one side.[13]

When Bill Flemings died, his funeral was held at the old Clover Hill Methodist Church. Hiram Whitmer stayed around after the graveside service until no one was left but the grave diggers. They lowered the casket into the ground, then picked up their shovels to fill the grave. Hiram removed his coat, took one of the shovels and said, "Would you mind?" He then helped to bury his friend.[14]

Old Rufus

Glick's Foundry, just east of the village of Montezuma, over on the Dry River Road, was one of Rockingham County's busiest hives of industry. There was a blacksmith shop there, a flour mill, a cider mill, a hominy mill and an apple butter boiling shed, all standing at the edge of a large mill pond.

The Brethren used to baptize people in the pond at all times of the year. One January, around the year 1900, there was a gathering for the baptism of old Rufus Hildebrand. The crowd of observers was unusually large, for this was a very special occasion, one they thought would be well worth witnessing.

No one had thought to see the day when Rufus Hildebrand would humble himself before anyone, much less the Lord. He had lived his life according to his own terms, and while he was not considered an evil man, he was nonetheless thought to be a prize candidate for redemption.

As his family looked on with pride and his cronies shook their heads in disbelief, Rufus and the minister made their way out into the cold, cold water. They were about thigh deep when Rufus began to imagine the dunking that was soon to come. He shivered and asked the minister, "Couldn't we wait and do this when the weather warms up a bit?"

The preacher responded with a question of his own. "What if you die before then?" Rufus turned and made his way back to the shore. He called back over his shoulder, "Oh, the Lord has waited this long. I think he'll wait 'til spring."[15]

The Pitcher
Circa 1908

My grandfather, the first John L. Heatwole, was a no-nonsense businessman who left the Valley and the farm with some bitterness when he was in his mid-thirties.

While he was still in his early teens, his mother suffered a stroke and his father was incapacitated by typhoid fever. When his older brother married and moved away, he was left to look after his parents, his grandfather and five brothers and sisters. With all the farm chores and his schoolwork, he hardly had any time for himself. His only escape from all of his responsibilities was baseball.

John L. Heatwole (1890-1980)
The Clover Hill curve ball ace

In the spring and summer he was in his glory—he pitched for the Clover Hill team, and they were the club to beat. It was said that in the weeks before the national baseball season started, a few professional players, traveling incognito, would come to Rockingham to try to hit off of John Heatwole.

As far as it went, it was a nice story, but in 1975 my Uncle Paul, grandfather's younger brother, elaborated and sent it into the realm of legends. My grandfather, he told me, was famous for his curve ball. "That ball," he said, "would almost reach the plate when it would break to the right and go behind the batter's back—and *then* the batter swung."[16] I had to laugh. This, I thought, was surely one of the all-time great tall tales.

A few months later, my grandfather came to the Valley on one of his infrequent visits. The three of us were sitting around the kitchen table one night when I remembered that outlandish baseball story and decided to have some fun at Uncle Paul's expense.

Grandfather was a literal man and had no patience with make-believe or embellishment. Once he had fixed the truth or falseness of a remark in his mind, he would argue his position for hours and never back down. I'd often heard him snort in disbelief or utter something like, "If you believe that ...," or "Come on now, Paul, do you expect us to ...," after hearing one of his brother's yarns.

Anyway, I told my grandfather Uncle Paul's story about his prowess as a baseball pitcher. He nodded in agreement as I repeated the story of the professional players, but when I got to the part about the curve ball, I expected an outburst of derision. Instead, a distant look of memory came into his eyes, and he said, "Yep, I could do that."

I was absolutely dumbfounded!

"I could have turned professional," he said, "but one morning I was milking a cow, and she kicked me in the elbow. I was never able to throw like that again."

Ben Southard

Ben Southard's blacksmith shop stood on the north bank of Dry River just up from Rushville School and the village. He was what most people think of when a blacksmith comes to mind—big, strong, moustached and reliable. He loved life and was a great storyteller. He was also the subject of wonderful stories during his lifetime.

Ben made up his own business slogan:

> If you want your horse
> shod to pace and trot
> Get him shod
> at B. F. Southard's Shop

It was his boast that he could "shoe anything that wears a tail."[17]

While at work in the forge, Ben always kept an ear open for the sound of the children down at the Rushville School being let out for the day. He knew they would run up to the open door of the shop and expect Ben to put on a show for them—and they were never disappointed.

Ben Southard, the Rushville blacksmith

As the children filled the doorway, Ben bellowed up the heat in the forge until a bar of iron was red-hot. Then he removed the bar from the coals with tongs, spit on the cold anvil, placed the glowing bar where the spit was and struck the bar with the hammer.

The result was a brilliant shower of sparks that shot off in all directions. In the dim interior of the shop, it looked like a Fourth of July celebration to the delighted schoolchildren.[18]

When Ben needed to shoe a horse and a loafer was hanging around the shop, he'd put him to work. He'd have the visitor hold up one of the front legs, and he'd go back and shoe the opposite rear hoof. By doing it that way, the horse was off balance and couldn't kick.[19]

Ben loved to hunt squirrels with his tomcat named Belshazzar, after the king in the Bible who "saw the handwriting on the wall." It's well known that while a hunter is taking aim, a squirrel will usually move to the far side of the tree. As the hunter changes position, it is likely the squirrel will also. Ben avoided all of this maneuvering around the tree by training Bel to climb about halfway up toward the squirrel. When the squirrel saw Bel, it froze in place, and Ben could get off a clean shot without all of the aggravation.[20]

Once, a fellow saw a rifle that Ben owned and took a powerful shine to it. He said if Ben was willing to sell, he was in the market to buy if the price was right. Now Ben Southard was a sharp salesman. He said he'd consider selling, but first he had to tell him about the gun's special feature. "You got to put salt in the barrel before you fire it."

The prospective buyer was baffled and asked why that should be done.

"Well," said Ben, "this gun shoots so far and so accurate that you got to use salt so the meat won't spoil before you can get to it."[21]

Ben had a brother-in-law who could never get into a business venture without losing his shirt. This brother-in-law came by Ben's home one day and made him a proposition. "Ben, you're the salesman in the family. Purina has this new laying mash for chickens. If you'll sell it for me, you don't have to put a nickel in it, and you can have half the profits."

They struck the bargain, and Ben went to work. After closing the blacksmith shop, he loaded the wagon with sacks of the new product and went from farm to farm. When the farmer answered the door, Ben introduced himself, as if they didn't already know him.

"I'm Ben Southard, and I represent the Purina folks. They have this great new laying mash. You mix it up with your regular chicken feed. The chickens take a bite of it, tighten up their lips, curl up their toes, and fill the atmosphere with eggs!" He returned home with an empty wagon and a full purse.[22]

Glick's Foundry was on the road that left Montezuma and followed the fields along Dry River going up toward Clover Hill and Lilly. When Ben heard that the mill at the foundry complex had burned to the ground, he could not resist saying, "there's a dam by a mill site but not a mill by a damn sight."[23]

Ben couldn't abide the mistreatment of animals. In 1917 he visited Wray, Colorado, where his son Charlie had gone to work as a cowboy. While he was there, one day he saw a man beating a dog in the dusty street. He grabbed the man by the shirtfront with one hand and lifted him up so that only his toes touched the ground. The old blacksmith shook him violently while exclaiming, "before you can whip a dog, you've got to have more sense than the dog!" [24]

Jasper Smith's store in Rushville was always a favorite gathering place for people from the surrounding countryside. For years Ben Southard and several of his friends showed up at the store on Saturday evenings to play music. Ben was the group's leader, and his fiddle playing was much admired. The only drawback to playing at the store was that it didn't have space for much of a crowd. Some people were left outside listening in at the doors and windows.

That all changed in the mid-1890s, when the telephone came to and took root in southwestern Rockingham County. Ben saw this event as a golden opportunity to reach a wider audience. As usual, he and the band showed up at the store one night. With Jasper Smith's permission, Ben picked up the store's telephone receiver and cranked out the "eleven shorts" emergency signal. He knew that everyone along the line would pick up to see what was going on.

"Hello," he said, "no emergency, folks, just Ben Southard and the boys down at Smith's Store. Would you like to hear some good music?" Everyone responded with enthusiasm. This could have been the first live "broadcast" of music in the nation.[25]

Walking home one day Ben saw an old man—he was about 70 years old—cutting wood and crying. Ben stopped and asked him why he was crying, and the old man sniffed, "cause my pa whipped me."

Somewhat surprised, Ben blurted out, "You mean your father is still living?" The old fella nodded.

"What did he whip you for?"

The old man wiped away his tears and answered, "Fer sassin' my granddaddy." It was said that this man's grandfather was so old he'd hardly ever move from his porch chair. He sat there so long that the grape vines grew around him.[26]

Reed's Painless Tooth Removal Service

Old Dave Reed, the shoemaker of the village of Clover Hill, was a Confederate veteran. His experiences in the army made him a firm believer in his ability to master any situation.

The most famous story that circulated about him in western Rockingham County concerned his wife's awful toothache. It came on her suddenly in the night. She heated a kettle of tea over the fire and poured the steaming liquid onto a folded towel. When he awoke the next morning, Dave found her holding the towel against her inflamed jaw as she jerked around the room, beside herself with pain. It was obvious that the compress was not drawing away any of the agony she was contending with.

Her husband had to do some tall talking to get her to open her mouth so he could see the offending tooth. She made him first promise not to touch it. He had no difficulty in seeing it. Later he swore he could see it throbbing.

He told his wife that it would have to come out before she'd have any relief. She was terrified at the thought of having a tooth pulled, but Dave promised her that he could remove it without her feeling any pain. His preparations were complicated. He made her sit in a chair just opposite the closed front door, where he left her while he jammed an iron poker into the glowing coals of the fireplace.

In a wall cupboard he located some waxed linen thread that was used in shoe cobbling. He knew it was tough and suited his purpose. When he explained that he wanted to tie a loop around the troublesome tooth, she resisted. He promised her that he would not yank it, and again assured her that if she would trust him, she would feel no pain. He cautioned her to keep her eyes closed and to open her mouth as wide as possible.

He tied the line securely around the offending tooth, then he played it out and tied the other end to the doorknob. Tiptoeing across the room, he removed the red-hot poker from the fire. His wife still had her eyes tightly shut as he quietly came to her side.

Almost simultaneously, he thrust the poker close under her nose, she jerked her head back, and the tooth flew from her mouth and rattled to the foot of the door.

The method wasn't exactly painless, but it was fast. And that, because of his wife's excruciating pain, was the important consideration in Dave Reed's mind.[27]

Honored Guest

There lived in Strasburg in the 19th century a greatly admired and much loved traveling evangelist and circuit preacher known far and wide as Brother Haymaker. He went back into the mountains to visit isolated settlements and farms, bringing the gospel and news of the outside world with him. His journeys took him through the Blue Ridge and across the Valley into the Allegheny Front.

The people looked forward to his visits with marked anticipation. Cabins and rickety, weather-beaten frame houses were cleaned and aired and a room was prepared for Brother Haymaker to spend the night. He was always treated as an honored guest. Nothing was too good for Brother Haymaker.

While staying over with one mountain family, he retired for the night after a long day of caring for the spiritual needs of his hosts. Early the next morning he was called to breakfast, but he wasn't quite ready to get up. He turned over and went back to sleep.

Soon he was called again, and he grumpily asked over his shoulder what all the hurry was about. From the opposite side of the door came an answer that was nothing he ever expected.

"Well," said the voice with some hesitancy, "we want that sheet you're on there for a tablecloth."[28]

Escapade

Leo Huffman left school at sixteen to help out full-time on his family's 240-acre farm in western Augusta County. Though his labors were many, his mind and sense of fun remained active.

One sharp, crisp winter day, Leo's mother and father had business in the nearby town of Fordwick. They left Leo to haul manure from the barn, but they hadn't been gone long when Leo's thoughts turned to ice skating. He put the horses back in the barn and hurried to the house. He decided that it was best that he go in disguise, so he donned his mother's old long dress, her old coat and her old slat bonnet. Grabbing his skates, he ran from the house and rode off down the road on his bicycle, skirts flapping.

The pond was about a half mile from his home. His old school stood on a rise just above it. The ice was in good shape, and Leo executed some fancy figures. When he chanced to look up at the school, he saw the students and their teachers at the windows. They were obviously amazed at the old lady's skill and dash.

After he had satisfied his need for self and community entertainment, he removed the skates and pedaled back down the road. On the way he overtook a neighbor, Mr. Taylor, who was driving a wagonload of flour pulled by two mules. Since he was still in his mother's clothes, he decided to have some fun with the old man.

Leo drew alongside and gestured wildly for the wagon to stop. Mr. Taylor was startled, thinking that the old woman must be insane. Leo jumped off his bicycle and tried to get on the wagon, but Mr. Taylor whipped the mules to a gallop.

Leo had a good laugh, then returned home, changed out of his costume and got back into his own clothes. Soon he was back at work with the chore his parents had set him.

Meanwhile, the distraught Mr. Taylor arrived in Fordwick, two miles distant. He went into the store where Leo's mother and father were shopping and told the Huffmans that there was a crazy woman down the road near their place.

Mr. Taylor was so shaken that he thought the incident was important enough to relay to Officer Palmer. He found the policeman down the street and told him about the crazy woman. Palmer hunted up his deputy, and the two men drove their buggy out to the Huffman farm. They didn't encounter anyone along the way.

When they arrived at the farm, they found Leo hard at work shoveling manure out of the barn. They approached him and asked, "Boy, did you see a crazy woman down here?"

Leo answered, "Yes, I saw her," as he lowered his head.

"Where did she go?"

The boy looked a little sheepish and after a moment spoke quietly. "Do you see that graveyard over on the hill?"

Office Palmer looked hard at Leo for a long minute, and then said directly to him, "That is the place she ought to be."

The officers got back in their buggy and drove off.

When his parents returned, they asked Leo what had been going on. He couldn't lie to them, and told them about his grand escapade.

Leo, who came by his sense of humor honestly, was joined by his mother and father in another good laugh.[29]

Retribution in Page County

One hot Sunday morning, years and years ago, a boy named Herman decided to skip out on the long sermon that he knew would be offered at the Lutheran church. The church stood on a broad hill at the edge of Deacon Smith's field, and below it was the best swimming hole in the county. There is nothing better than a swim in the spring branch on a sweltering morning, and Herman knew it.

He waited in hiding until the last of the congregation entered the building, then made his way to the old swimming hole. He removed all of his clothes and was preparing to jump in when he heard an ominous noise behind him. He turned his head and to his horror saw the deacon's vicious bull bearing down on him with murder flashing in his eyes. The boy hardly had time to think. Leaving his clothes in a pile on the ground, he ran as fast as his legs could carry him. The boy dodged this way and that, but the bull stayed close on his heels.

The bull had never been known to be in that particular field before, but now here he was, apparently out to kill an innocent boy whose only sin was skipping church services.

At one point Herman made a particularly good cut, and the bull passed him. Herman grabbed the beast's tail as he flashed by and ran along behind. He hoped he could wear the enraged bull down and at the same time avoid the terrifying horns.

Suddenly, miracle of miracles, the bull stopped under a broad, spreading oak tree. The boy jumped for a low branch and swung himself up and in, thinking he was safe at last. But God wasn't finished with Herman just yet. On a higher limb there was a large nest of hornets that had been jolted when Herman bounded to his perch. They came after him with a vengeance.

After being stung several times, he made a drastic decision—the only one open to him. The bull was standing directly below him and Herman, in a desperate attempt to escape the angry hornets, dropped to the bull's back and held on for dear life.

At that point God brought matters to a dramatic close. The bull took off up the hill, toward the church, where services were just letting out, with the naked boy clutching his horns. The bull let out a ferocious bellow, and instantly, it seemed, the whole congregation was watching in splendid fascination.

Luckily for the spectators, the churchyard was enclosed by a stout fence; the bull made right for it. It seemed as if he'd leap the barrier, but he turned abruptly to the left, pitching Herman, in all his glory, right over the fence—where he landed in the soft grass at the feet of family, friends and neighbors.

It's a shame that a copy of the sermon preached the next Sunday has not been preserved.[30]

All Innocence

When Dwight Shull was about four years old he was taken back into Wise Hollow by his mother to meet her uncle, Henry Shull. Henry lived up in a side hollow in Augusta County, just over the line from Rockingham County. His home was a large old log cabin built by his Kersh ancestors.

Dwight and his mother entered the room where Henry sat rocking. His mother prompted the boy, "Why don't you say hello to your Uncle Hen?"

Dwight, in all innocence, looked up at his mother and asked, "Does he lay eggs?"[31]

Kate Shank Blosser

Obituaries sometimes convey fascinating and unusual stories. The history of Kate Shank Blosser, who passed away on July 17, 1932, at the age of 77, is a case in point. When she was born in 1855 into Rockingham County's Mennonite community, she weighed only one and a half pounds. In an age before the invention of life support systems for premature or frail infants, it is remarkable that she lived. She must have been the talk of the county.

Kate was so small that a grain of corn could cover the palm of her hand, and a half dollar could hide her face. It was related that she could be placed in a quart crock and covered with a hand. Until she was six months old, she was carried about on a pillow. At nine years of age, she weighed only thirty-seven and a half pounds.

She grew to be a healthy woman and survived all of her brothers and sisters in a family of nine. Kate was married twice, was the mother of fifteen children and was survived by eighty grandchildren and eighteen great-grandchildren. She is buried in the cemetery of the Pike Mennonite Church south of Harrisonburg.[32]

If It Pleases ...

Charles Curry, who grew up in the Hills of Judea in Augusta County was quite a character. For many years he practiced law in Staunton, where his unorthodox methods were the source of great amusement in the community.

On one occasion he was assigned by the court to defend a man accused of stealing a ham. In the pre-trial interview at the man's home, Mr. Curry asked his client if he had indeed stolen the item in question. The simple fellow answered without hesitation that he had done the deed. Mr. Curry thought it over for awhile before saying, "Well, you give me half of that ham." This was done.

When the case came before the court, Mr. Curry, on behalf of his client, requested a trial by jury. Once the prosecution stated its position, Mr. Curry rose to his feet and addressed the jury directly. "Gentlemen," he said, "this man doesn't have any more of that ham than I do." Not guilty was the verdict delivered.[33]

In a personal injury case at another time, Mr. Curry instructed a client to say that he was unable to lift his arm above shoulder level. During the hearing, the opposing lawyer asked Mr. Curry's client to show the court the extent of his handicap. The man raised his arm to shoulder height, as instructed by his own attorney. The lawyer then quickly slipped in another question. "Now, how far could you lift it before the accident?"

Without thinking, the man raised his arm high over his head. Mr. Curry groaned and lowered his head to the counsel table.[34]

Poet of Pineville

A certain teacher at the Pineville school was disliked immensely by one of the boys, who wrote this poem on the outside of the school building:

> An eagle flew north to south
> And carried Fannie Larman in his mouth.
> When he found he had a fool,
> He dropped her in the Pineville School.[35]

Hot Roman Nights

Near the hamlet of Roman, in Augusta County, two sets of people awaited the end of the world on a couple of different occasions around the end of the 19th century.

The first was a group of "radical" Mormons who had moved into the area. Their leader had alienated a lot of local people with his ravings about the imminent coming of Judgment Day. Nonetheless, he had converted a few of the natives. He appointed an evening when the Lord would come and take the faithful to heaven as he destroyed the rest of the world.

There was a huge haymow near the hamlet; the Mormons put a ladder against it, and the believers climbed on top to await the end. There were about a dozen of them. Two teenage boys crept up to the mow in the dusk and struck matches as the devout prayed above them. Soon flames were licking up two sides of the stack. The boys ran for cover and watched with great glee as the Mormons came tumbling off the mound.

Somehow the boys were identified, brought before the magistrate and were found guilty of arson. They were each fined fifty cents. The Mormons soon moved away, hoping to find a friendlier reception elsewhere.

Another story says that two men were on a haystack waiting for the world to end and that they fell to sleep. In this case also, someone lighted the hay afire. As the men awoke to the smoke and flames, one of them exclaimed, "In hell, just as I expected!"[36]

What the Snake Knew

The late Elmer Byrd of Bridgewater used to tell a story of a fight he witnessed between a large blacksnake and an equally large rattlesnake.

The battle took place on a path a little up the mountain from Rawley Springs in Rockingham County.

Elmer was standing off in the woods when the two snakes met on the path. He said that it seemed as if both snakes stood about four feet tall on the ends of their tails. They swayed back and forth and sized each other's strength before suddenly striking. The blacksnake broke off the struggle for a moment and went to the side of the path and chewed on the leaves of a small plant growing there; he then returned to the combat. Every time the blacksnake was bitten, he repeated his first action of stopping to chew on a plant near the scene.

Finally, after what seemed the best part of an hour, the blacksnake prevailed and killed the deadly rattlesnake. Looking none the worse for wear, the victor glided off into the forest. Elmer retrieved the rattler and took it home to skin it for its beautifully patterned hide.

Later, when he thought back to the snake fight, he remembered the queer behavior of the blacksnake. He figured that the plant the snake had chewed on must have contained antibodies that protected it from the rattler's poison.

As soon as he had a chance, he returned to the mountain and tried to find the site of the struggle, but he never could. Many times he was heard to say, "I could have been a rich man today if I'd a paid attention to what that blacksnake was a chewin' on!"[37]

What the Snake Didn't Know

An interesting thing about snakes is that they swallow their food whole. The meal is slowly broken down in the reptile's digestive system. A favorite food of snakes that can't be digested in the usual manner is the egg. After swallowing an egg whole, a snake must find a narrow space to slither through, which breaks the egg inside.

In Augusta County a farmer's wife was having trouble with a snake that visited her hen house nightly, stealing eggs and terrorizing the chickens. The building was riddled with small holes and cracks a snake could use to enter and exit by. The woman wasn't about to lose several night's sleep trying to find and do away with the snake. Being sensible, as most farm folks are, she came up with a fail-proof plan.

It was high summer and the woman found a small gourd the size and shape of an egg. She painted it with whitewash and set it in a nest.

Within a few days her idea paid off. Going out one morning she found the snake firmly wedged in a crack in a wall board. The snake must have been surprised when the "egg" inside it refused to break. In trying harder to draw the supposed egg through the crusher, the snake had gotten stuck and saw its career end as the farm woman swung the axe.[38]

"I Swear!"

Nineteenth century magistrates in the Shenandoah Valley were empowered by law to arbitrate local disputes and to send certain cases to the county court if the circumstances warranted.

Once, in Shenandoah County, a poor widow came to the local magistrate, Squire Levi Cullers, with a problem. She only had one hog and she was counting on the meat to get her family through the next winter. The hog had gotten out of its pen and mingled with a neighbor's stock of hogs. When she went to the neighbor and asked for the return of her animal, which she said she could identify, he refused to turn it over.

Squire Cullers told her that if she would swear as to which hog was hers, she could have it back. The widow knitted her brows in consternation, then finally replied, "Well, now, I sure do hate to swear, but I need the meat, and damned if it isn't my hog!"

The squire chuckled and accompanied the woman to retrieve her property.[39]

The Birds

Early in the 20th century, near the lovely village of Singers Glen in Rockingham County, there lived a very mean old man. How mean was he? He was so mean that his favorite pastime was to sit on his front porch and shoot every bird that alighted on the fence that separated his yard from the road. He didn't care if the bird was a crow or a cardinal, a bluejay or a dove—he shot them all. For years he killed every bird that was unfortunate enough to select that particular fence to rest upon.

Well, eventually the old man came to his own end. His body was removed from the house and prepared for burial, and on the day of the funeral, following the church service, his casket was carried down the road toward the cemetery. As the procession approached the dead man's house, everyone plainly saw that his fence, for so long an execution site, was lined thickly with birds bearing witness to a terrible enemy's passing.[40]

Games, Pastimes & Special Events

Before twentieth century distractions came into the country, people took their entertainment when and where they could find it or create it. Events that seem commonplace to us today were sources of treasured memories to people whose existence was centered around hard work.

Life on the farm or in the mountains was mostly predictable, with daily routines dictated by the weather and the changing seasons. All over the Valley, huckleberry picking was a mid to late August summer ritual. The pickers ate the delicious berries right off the bushes, fresh huckleberry pies, muffins and cobblers were baked, and many berries were dried for later use. Each picker had his own secret patches in the hills and mountains that were harvested year after year.

Berry picking wasn't pure fun, though. Huckleberry patches are a favorite haunt of snakes. Pickers cut an onion in half and rubbed it over their hands and arms to repel the reptiles.[1]

The simple act of going to town was an adventure for both young and old. Trips to a good-sized town ten or twenty miles distant were taken only a couple of times a year, if that often; some people didn't go for years at a stretch. Those journeys were day-long affairs and often occasioned staying away from home overnight. In between these rare treks, any opportunity to visit with neighbors was eagerly seized upon. Church services, weddings, funerals, school activities, communal harvesting and pick-up and organized games were all of great interest.

Some of the old games are similar to ones we know today, although they were often more colorful, and some were obviously early courting rituals. Today there are so many activities contending for our attention that we condense diversions in order to fit games into our schedules. Conversely, past generations used the games to break up and take their minds away from the unrelenting daily cycles of life. Their free time was difficult to come by, so they made the most of all occasions.

Fox Hunt

At the Brady Schoolhouse, a one-room building near Fulks Run in Rockingham County, children had an hour for recess, regardless of the weather. When it snowed, a favorite game there was a reverse form of tag called Fox Hunt. One child, a hearty soul, was chosen to be the fox; all of the other children were the hounds. The fox was given a five-minute head start. Because of the snow you'd think the fox would be easy to track, but here craftiness came into the play. The fox child used brush piles, downed trees, creeks and anything else it could to break up and mask the trail. The pack had to stay together in the pursuit. The longer it lasted, the more fun it was.[2]

Eating lunch was secondary to playing games with schoolmates. At the Pine Knot School, down the road from Pineville in eastern Rockingham, an informant related the importance of recess. "We lived near school, so we went home for lunch. We'd swallow our lunch whole so we could get back to school to play."[3]

Tap the Rabbit

Tap the Rabbit was a game played by children in the Mount Sidney area of Augusta County and also along Dry River in Rockingham. They stood in a big ring, facing inward, and a designated child would prowl about behind their backs, outside the ring. He'd tap a child on the shoulder and then take off as fast as he could, trying to circumnavigate the ring. The tapped child would pursue, trying to tag the first child before he got all the way around to the tapped child's vacated space. If he didn't make the tag, he became the new "it."[4]

Another informant described the game as being played in the snow, with the circle being about thirty feet in diameter. The variant was that if you were caught by the person you tapped, you had to give him or her a kiss.[5]

Drop the Handkerchief

Drop the Handkerchief is variant of Tap the Rabbit that was played in the Old Order Mennonite community near the town of Dayton in Rockingham County. A player had to be extremely fast to succeed in this version. Instead of tapping someone on the shoulder, a handkerchief was dropped behind him. There was probably a lot of neck craning involved. The player had to wheel around, pick up the bit of cloth and try to catch the person who had dropped it.[6]

Balancing Act

All over the Valley a game of personal challenge for children was to see how long and how far you could walk balancing yourself on the top rail of a fence.[7]

Squirrelly

Squirrelly was a game played in both Augusta and Rockingham counties and probably elsewhere in the Valley. It likely took the place of common tag when members of the opposite sex first began to take serious notice of one another. The rules were just like tag, except that in Squirrelly "it" got to kiss the person caught. Players either moved very fast or not fast enough, depending on their interest in catching or in being caught.[8]

Stray Goose

Stray Goose was a running and hiding game in Augusta County that covered a great area. The children divided up into two teams, usually three or four to a side. One team was designated as the geese. Both sides would spread way out. At a given signal, the geese would scatter in all directions, yelling "stray goose!" The members of the other team pursued them until all the geese were tagged.

Once during a game, a stray goose "ran hard into a clothes line and was laid out flat; we caught him pretty easy."[9]

Barnyard Rodeo

"When we were down in the grades, we had to entertain ourselves. Out in the barnyard we would corner a calf or a colt that had never been tied. We'd get 'em over into a fence corner and one of us would jump on board from above. It could be right wild, that ride. If you didn't hold on tight, you'd soon land down there in the manure and all. We didn't fight the real mean ones."[10]

Love in the Dark

Love in the Dark was a favorite game played along Dry River by teenagers. It was similar to the mid-20th-century kissing game Post Office. A boy and a girl were put in a pitch dark room without having seen each other. They disguised their voices and talked awhile, hugged a little, and exchanged a kiss or two while trying to guess who they were with.[11]

Annie Over

Annie Over was played in Augusta County and was probably played in other areas under a different name. It was simple: two people, one on each side of a building, each threw a ball over it. If the person on the other side caught it, he could sneak or run around and try to hit you with it. If you got around the corner of the building before being hit, or if the ball missed you, he'd have to go back to his original side. If you were hit, you'd have to change sides.[12]

In Clarke County, the children at the one-room Pine Corner School played Annie Over during recess. They chose up sides, six or eight or even more on a team, and the ball was thrown over the school. The one who caught the ball tried to tag or hit one of the opposing players with it before they escaped around the corner. The person hit or tagged changed sides. When recess was over, the team with the most people was the winner.[13]

Poor Pussy Wants a Corner

Poor Pussy Wants a Corner was a house game played in both Augusta and Rockingham counties. Five people were needed to play, and a good-sized room with little furniture in it. One person stood in the middle of the room and one in each corner. When the child in the middle called out, "Poor pussy wants a corner," everyone had to run to a different corner. If the middle child beat one of the others to a new corner, that child had to go to the middle. The object was to remain a corner child.[14]

Old Order Mennonites played the same game with a slight variation. The child in the middle would turn to one side of the room and say in a sad voice, "Poor pussy wants a corner," and then would turn and do the same to the other side. When the middle child had his or her back turned, the children behind might seize the opportunity to change corners with each other. The child in the middle had to be especially watchful.[15]

In eastern Rockingham County, Poor Pussy Wants a Corner was sometimes played on a porch. The columns on the porch took the place of corners in a room. A door could also be designated a corner. In this variation, more than five children could play.[16]

Fox in the Morning

Fox in the Morning was played with two bases about one hundred yards apart. Two teams, about three people on each, would stand on their base. One team would be designated "it," and they would try to keep the other team's members from getting to their base by tagging them out. The other team could run all over the place dodging tags while trying to get on their opponents' base. As members of the invading side were tagged out and changed sides, the numbers of those in pursuit increased.[18]

In the Mt. Clinton area of Rockingham County, the game was prefaced with a taunting chant hurled back and forth between the teams:

> Fox in the morning;
> goose and the gander;
> How many comes out?
> more than you can handle!"[19]

Shinny

The game Shinny was played like field hockey. A ball was hit with a long paddle-like stick, and there were two goals to be defended. The twist was that if you normally hit the ball on your right side, you had to hit left and vice-versa if you were left handed. If you forgot and switched back to your normal hitting position to strike the ball, a player on the other team could smack you freely on the shin as a penalty.[17]

Baseball

Everyone played baseball in both pick-up and organized form. Great rivalries sprang up between villages, towns and country schools; some continue to this day. Back then they played almost year 'round.

One game in the early 20th century was played in Squire Tom Heatwole's field along Dry River between teams from the Franklin School and the Rushville School. It was a very cold day in the late fall. The *News Record* of Harrisonburg covered the contest, which was won by Rushville. At the end of their article they noted: "hard to understand this winter baseball."[20]

Spot Tag

Spot Tag must have been hilarious to watch as it progressed from one child to another. It was played like traditional tag for the most part, but what made it different was that when a person was tagged, he had to hold a hand to the place where he was touched. He was then "it" and had to pursue the next victim, holding his "spot" as he ran.

If a child were tagged low, like on an ankle, it could be very difficult for him. Imagine being tagged on the back of the neck and having to chase the other children with a hand clapped on that spot. This was a simple and wonderful game.[21]

Put 'n Take

Playing marbles was not only a pastime but something akin to a ritual for boys in years past. In the 19th century, a new item was introduced that made the playing of the game secondary to the quick acquisition of the marbles themselves. This was a small top called a Put 'n Take. It was variously made from solid brass, hollow brass, hollow silver, celluloid or wood. Most were six- or eight-sided and were marked with letters and numbers to signify what the player was required to do after having spun the top.

The game was started with each player putting in a marble to make up the initial pot. One boy was chosen to spin his Put 'n Take. As long as the side of the top that was up when it stopped told him to take from the pot, he stayed in control. The T above a number meant take that many; a TA meant "take all," and then everyone put up another marble. When he got a P, a "put" side, or an AP, "all put," he lost control and another player spun his own Put 'n Take.

Some Put 'n Takes had a circle and a star on two of their flats instead of letters. The circle indicated "all put" and the star "take all."

"Put 'n Takes" made from brass, silver and celluloid.

Vast fortunes of marbles were won or lost during recess or on a lazy summer afternoon. The use of Put 'n Takes faded in the early 20th century. Until then almost every boy carried one in his pocket or marble bag.[22]

Catch the Gray Wolf

Backcountry "hide and go seek" was called "catch the grey wolf."[23]

Christmas Traditions

Christmas was celebrated with oranges, raisins, candy and baked goods. Prized gifts might be drums, a hand-made doll, or a toy horse and wagon. Neighbors visited and, if the weather cooperated, they'd get up a game of croquet on the lawn; there was an indoor version for blustery days. Santa

Claus was not yet a part of the holiday ritual.[24]

In the Pineville area of Rockingham County around 1900, fire-crackers and Roman candles were set off on Christmas eve. Children of the Ritenour family received an orange, a stick of candy and a small toy on Christmas morning and were thrilled.[25]

Some people put up a tree, and others decorated with pine branches and garlands. Cranberries and popcorn strung by children made the home festive. Everyone looked forward to Christmas supper. For some celebrants chicken was a delight, while others chose turkey or a goose.[26]

Christmas in Town

Christmas celebrations in town were very different from those in the country. Around 1880 in Staunton, the county seat for Augusta County, the economy was still depressed because of the Civil War, but people did the best they could to get into the spirit of the season. Some of the churches put up decorated trees, but most of the town residents did not. The folks of German ancestry illuminated their trees with small tallow candles. Gifts were distributed on Christmas Eve. The children were told that they had been brought by *Christkindlein* (the Christ child).

Most of the adult population observed Christmas Day with church, feasting and partaking of the goodness of the wassail bowl. Another element celebrated a bit too much in the thirteen bar rooms then operating in Staunton. The police didn't get a holiday—it was their duty to keep an eye on the revelers.

Fire-crackers were an accepted part of Christmas. Small fire-crackers, called squibs, came all the way from China and cost five cents for fifty. Cracker shooting began at about 6 P.M. on Christmas Eve, and the town was bedlam for about an hour; it started up again on Christmas Day.

Two brothers in Staunton made a large tin horn measuring ten feet long with a fifteen-inch diameter bell on the end. These were very accomplished young men. The sound of the horn could be heard blocks away, and the people loved it.[27]

Belsnickling

Belsnickling was a longtime Christmas tradition in the Valley brought in by the early Pennsylvania Dutch settlers. People dressed up in old clothes, wore false faces and masks, and went to visit their neighbors thus attired. The girls went out during the day, and the boys went out at night. They made a racket as they approached a house, sometimes even firing guns into the air. They disguised their voices, and if those they visited could not identify them, they were invited inside. There they would remove their masks and be treated to cider or punch and cookies.[28]

One informant recalled with evident pleasure that "the most fun about *Belsnickling* was trying to guess who was behind the mask."[29] It must also be said that the practice was frowned on by some segments of the community who thought it harkened back to pagan celebrations.[30]

New Year's Day

The New Year was brought in with a bang of monumental proportions in the Port Republic area of Rockingham County. It was called "anvil shooting."

Young men carried two blacksmith's anvils into a field. The first one was placed upside down. The hollow pocket in its base was filled with gunpowder, and a fuse was inserted in it. The second anvil was stacked right-side-up on top of the first one.

The fuse was lighted, and everyone ran for their lives. There would soon be an explosion that made everything within a country mile tremble. It was enough to make the New Year wake up and take notice.[31]

Easter

At Easter there was a popular game called egg picking or egg fighting. Each player had a hard-boiled egg and challenged other players to tap eggs. The player whose eggshell cracked had to hand it over and was out of the game. Sometimes boys carved wooden eggs and tried to paint them to look real. Some players thought they had a better chance with a brown egg, because its shell was thought to be harder than a white one.[32]

People in the country usually did not receive a new hat or new suit of clothes at Easter; that was more of a town tradition. Instead, they attended church services in the morning and spent the rest of the day visiting, playing games and hiding and hunting eggs. The highlight of the day was the much-anticipated egg eating contest.[33]

Fourth of July

The Fourth of July was celebrated with picnics, speeches and band concerts. Individual families had picnics, and towns organized community picnics. Bridgewater always put on a huge picnic in Lowman's Woods on Dry River. A band played the popular airs of the day, and singing groups would vie with one another for the crowd's approval. Farm children watched and listened from the edge of the grounds.[34]

Work Gatherings

The most sociable part of making apple butter in the fall was cutting up the apples. This chore was given to the young people, who went about it eagerly. They knew that when they finished, there would be games to play and plenty of good food to eat.[35] Along Dry River this cutting was called "snitsin." When they were finished, they played Fox in the Morning, Tap the Rabbit and Squirrelly.[36]

Apple cuttings were an opportunity to socialize with members of the opposite sex. At one of these cuttings, near Mole Hill just after the Civil War, John Coffman was partnered to a girl, "with such bright eyes." A few years later, he and the bright-eyed Elizabeth Heatwole were married.[37]

Sugaring Time

Back in the mountains, as the sap in the maples rose in the spring, it was collected and boiled down to make maple syrup. At one point in the cooking process there was an extra-thick, syrupy layer in the bottom of the kettle. Children were allowed to dip a little of this out, and they poured it into a cup of cold water, where it firmed up like a gum ball. The children loved the little bits of sweet candy and called them "clinkers."[38]

Rag Cutting

When women along Dry River in the late 19th century got together for rag cuttings, they usually spoke "Dutch." The rags they cut up were later made into braided rugs. On one rainy day, as a prank, a boy with the devil in him scrambled their overshoes on the porch.[39]

Quilting Bees

There were many quilting bees held in homes along the river. It was said that the Mennonites and the "River Brethren" (United Brethren who had picked up the Wesleyan emphasis of the Methodists—they shouldn't be confused with the Church of the Brethren), would not come together for this most social of gatherings but instead held separate parties. They came from the same anabaptist background, but the River Brethren gave up some of their earlier pacifist sentiments when they became loosely aligned with the United Methodists, which created a schism between the two communities.[40]

Barn Raisings

Barn raisings started at daybreak and went on until the light failed. There was a short break for the noon meal and a huge feast at quitting time. The frame of the barn was erected, and the owner took care of the finishing. The women worked as hard as the men. They carried water and cooked all day.[41]

Harvest

"Harvest was a festival; a big dinner was prepared and thirty or forty neighbors came and finished the harvest in a few hours."[42]

Oyster Suppers

Oyster suppers have been part of Valley life for as long as anyone living can remember. Hard-working farm families dreamed of oyster suppers while they tended the summer fields.

There was an annual oyster supper held at Mount Pisgah (pronounced PIZ-GEY) schoolhouse in Augusta County. It was held in October and November and always at night.

"People would come from all over, in T-models and with horses and buggies. My mother would heat bricks in the stove and wrap them in blankets. They'd be put on the floor of the buggy and our feet would be warm all the way up to the school."

The oysters were fried, and vegetables, potatoes and pickles were served on the side. The choice of drinks was limited to water and coffee, though some of the local rowdies would slip down to the nearby cider mill looking for some hard stuff. The interior of the schoolhouse was lighted with kerosene lamps. "It was kind of dim in there. You had to kind of feel to find your mouth."[43]

Court Days

Everyone looked forward eagerly to Court Days, especially the December Court. Country people came to town to take care of legal business, and some traded horses while others did their Christmas shopping. Some carried cheese and crackers to eat; dining at a restaurant was a very rare occurrence. Before they left, they bought candy for the trip home, lemon drops being a favorite in some circles.[44] Children left back on the farm anticipated the return of their father, who was sure to bring them candy.[45]

In 1820, vendors set up tables in front of the Rockingham County Court House. They spread white tablecloths and piled them high with ginger cakes. Kegs of non-alcoholic molasses beer were set up nearby. It was reported that jury members let their hats down on a line from a second story window of the court house to be filled with cakes and jugs of beer.[46]

The August Court was known as the Watermelon Court because wagonload after wagonload of plump, tasty melons lined the streets of the county seat.[47]

Not everyone could come to town on court days, so some of those who were able to shopped for their neighbors. Women purchased material for home sewing or tried to match fabric samples and ribbons.

On court day, all of Water Street in Harrisonburg, which was mostly "mud in those days," was devoted to horse trading and drinking—the saloons were along there. One man returned home with a horse he had sold earlier in the day and a seventy-five dollar profit, to boot!

Farmers backed their wagons up against the courthouse square for an open air market on that day.[48]

Sleigh Rides

In the winter, after a good snowfall, sleigh riding parties were held. "On a moonlit night we'd all pile in and sing hymn songs ridin' along."[49]

Revivals

Religious revivals were held on Sundays, and all denominations attended. The children argued religion the next day at school.[50] One young fellow rode his bicycle all the way to Harrisonburg one night, a ten-mile round trip over rutted back roads, to hear a celebrated traveling preacher named Gypsy Smith.[51]

After Sunday services at Salem Church in Augusta County, "all the young people would get together at Seawright Springs and sit around on the benches and talk.[52]

Circus

Going to town for the circus was a great outing. Paul Landes went with an uncle on the train from Mt. Sidney to Staunton to take in the John Robinson Circus when he was a small boy. They saw a street parade and took special interest in the Hippo Wagon, which had a pool built into it. After the parade they hopped aboard the streetcar and rode out to the fairgrounds, where the tents and side shows were set up.

While there, Paul saw old "Fightin' Bob" Misner. He was bent over with age, but still had plenty of spunk left in him. Somebody accused him of cutting some tent ropes out of meanness, and nearly cornered him. "I haven't cut any rope, but I'm cutting one now," he snarled, then pulled out a knife, slashed a rope near his side and sprang away. Someone threw a dirt clod after him and hit his stooped back, but he escaped.[53]

When the circus arrived, the children of Page County took to the summer hills with buckets and baskets to gather huckleberries, their part in a pact between them and the circus folk that had gone on as long as anyone could remember. As showtime neared, the children traded a gallon of huckleberries for a ticket and a bag of peanuts. The children got a wonderful treat as they watched the acrobats, clowns, arialists and exotic animals perform under the big top, but anyone who has tasted the delights of freshly picked huckleberries knows who got the best of the bargain.[54]

Lawn Parties

Lawn parties are still held in many parts of the Shenandoah Valley, and then, as now, they were affairs that lasted all day and well into the night.

Not everyone in the country had an ice cream freezer to crank out ice cream, but it was made in abundance for the lawn parties. If you wanted to get on the good side of a special girl, you might treat her to a dish of the dessert. One girl was so popular that she ate fifteen saucers of ice cream, purchased by her many would-be beaus.[55]

Spelling Bees

Spelling bees were very well attended and were thought to be as important in the mountain communities as they were in the towns. They were exciting events and people travelled long distances to attend them.

Debating clubs and singing groups also drew large audiences. Literary societies conducted dialogues on various topics, from the current direction of fiction writing in the United States to the merits of the Grange movement.[56] In 1894, the Literary Society of the Clover Hill School in Rockingham County debated the question: "Resolved that there are more attractions in California than in Virginia." About twenty scholars took part in the exercise. The Bridgewater newspaper reported that the outcome was "decided in the negative, which was eminently proper."[57]

Ice Skating and Sledding

Ice skating parties were formed as soon as the weather hardened the ponds and rivers sufficiently. Night skating, with bonfires on the banks, was beautiful to watch.

In a time when cash didn't flow very freely, especially for children, there were methods that could be used to acquire desired goods. Two boys along Dry River worked at making dried apple snits for a couple of months one fall. They sold them for six cents a pound at Sipe's General Store at the corner of College and Main Streets in Bridgewater and used the money to buy ice skates to use that coming winter.[58]

Sledding in those days was called "coasting."[59]

Camping

Family camping in the mountains was a pastime that was fondly remembered for years by all involved. Sometimes families stayed for weeks, hauling tents, food and cooking gear in open farm wagons. That was no mean feat, what with the rough roads and flowing streams to be crossed. They slung hammocks in the trees, and some folks even took feather ticks along for added comfort. Time passed lazily while they hiked, ate, played games, sang and read. They also took the opportunity to visit the boys who had been sent into the mountains for the summer to take care of cattle grazing there and resupply the boys' disappearing store of food.[60]

One informant's description of the journey to the mountains goes into wonderful detail. "They drove to Blacks Run with a two-horse wagon. There was always a chicken coop with young chickens, which they dressed as needed. They took all kinds of farm produce and fruits. It was a nice place for a vacation, although it was rough getting there. They had to ford the creek in thirteen places."[61]

The Springs

Most of the Valley counties had resort springs in the relatively cooler mountain areas that were used for summer vacations in much the same way as people in the tidewater took advantage of breezes from the Chesapeake Bay and Atlantic Ocean to relieve the heat of the season. The spring operations varied in size. A few were used by local families, while others catered to a clientele from Richmond, Baltimore, Washington, D.C., and other cities both north and south. There were springs that offered services to people on almost every level of the economic scale. Rockbridge Alum Springs (thirteen miles west of Lexington), Rawley Springs (eleven miles west of Harrisonburg), and Orkney Springs (twelve miles west of Mt. Jackson), each could accommodate from six hundred to eight hundred guests in simple but comfortable surroundings.

Smaller resorts, like Wilson Springs in Rockbridge County, Stribling Springs (thirteen miles northwest of Staunton), and Hopkins Springs (east of the Massanutten Mountain), were justly proud of small, comfortable hotels that served from forty to seventy guests.

Wilson Springs was a traditional vacation spot for farm families from all over Rockbridge County during the last two weeks of July in Victorian times. They arrived in wagons loaded down with bedding, chairs and provisions. Around a wide area called the green, the farmers built rough cabins to live in during their stays. There were twenty-five to thirty such dwellings on the grounds.

The sulphur spring from which the resort took its name was located on an island in the Maury River. It could be reached by a footbridge and was a nice place for a picnic. There was a platform near the green that was used for dances, and local fiddlers and banjo players were hired to play for evening revels. For those who took pleasure in bowling, there was a ten-pin alley. As at all the family resorts, young and old alike were addicted to lawn croquet. And for those whose nature was tuned to more solitary pursuits, there was always the option of long walks in a majestic sylvan setting. A large house, which still stands there, was used to board visitors and was referred to as the "hotel."[62]

In Rockingham County, there seem to have been many springs where privately-owned cottages predominated. Three that come readily to mind are Union Springs (five miles north of Rawley Springs), Bloomer Springs (in the Massanutten Mountain), and Sparkling Springs (at the base of Little North Mountain, two miles west of the village of Singers Glen).[63] Each of these had many things in common: people came to relax, drink or bathe in the mineral waters, read, play games, make business contacts, find romance or to recuperate from an illness.

Lucky was the boy who was released from farm chores for a month to visit his aunt's cottage at Sparkling Springs. There were games to play with other children off in the hills and vales, and everyone joined in the matches played on the croquet grounds in the early evening.[64]

At Stribling Springs, some people played games of chance in the casino on the hill, while others took trail rides on horses from the stables. In some years guests staged elaborate plays on the lawns, with men taking the female roles and vice versa.[65]

The visitors at Rawley Springs might be wrapped in the music of an open-air band concert while ladies took the waters and gentlemen visited the bar room. General Beauregard or another southern icon might be visiting at the moment, while young couples hiked up to Lover's Leap to catch the moon's rise.[66]

Union Springs was associated early on with Mennonite families. Some folks had their own cottage, but there was also a boarding house that could accommodate about twenty guests called "the hotel." Miss Kate Croushorn managed the hotel in the summer; the rest of the year she taught school. Her sisters, Margaret and Lydia, worked their family farm a few miles down from the springs. They supplied the hotel with fresh produce.

Miss Kate hired a local boy each summer, and one season it was Bill Wheelbarger from down near the home farm. He had to care for the horses and saddle them up when the guests wanted to go riding, as well as attend to many other odd jobs around the place. He recalled that his main job was hauling water from a spring to the hotel.

Things were always busy, and it seemed as if every time he tried to take a breath, he'd be spotted by a guest and would be asked to run some errand. Miss Kate could always tell when one of her boys was being overwhelmed, and on one occasion she told Bill to "go to the barn and get lost. When I need you, I'll whistle for you." It was the only way he could get a break that summer.[67]

Other Valley families took advantage of the influx of visitors to Rawley Springs to earn a little extra money by

Mr. Fauver hamming it up at Stribling Springs circa 1890.

selling fresh garden produce to the kitchens. For the guests they took cantaloupes and watermelons and even jars of preserves, though some of these would break in transit because of the rough roads.[68]

Two farm girls, with the help of an aunt, devised a profitable scheme that city people couldn't resist—buying flowers from sweet country girls. "Aunt Sallie Jake made up the bunches. We sold them for her at 5¢ per bunch, and she gave us half the money. We thought we were rich. I saved all I earned one summer and bought material for Mattie and I each a dress, and enough material for brother Joe two dresses. He was around two years old. In those days boys wore dresses until they were five years old."[69]

Notable Contests

In Shenandoah County, near the town of New Market, there were held great and famous shooting matches. Men came from surrounding counties and from as far away as the mountain counties of Hardy and Pendleton in West Virginia. Many who participated in the competitions used long rifles made by Old Henry Spitzer in New Market decades before. Their owners bestowed names on the rifles that were famous among hunters and sportsmen, like Sun Perch, Old Mossey Creek, Bull of the Woods, Old Preacher, Black Snake and Old Fence Row. Prizes were turkeys and half and quarter beeves, but most competitors shot for honor.[70]

The Scots-Irish of the Hills of Judea held yearly assemblies at the Glen-Cose farm of George Glenn. Like the Scots Highlanders who settled in western North Carolina, these clannish men enjoyed testing their strengths and skills. They wrestled, boxed, jumped for distance, ran and went at it with sword and shillelagh. After all of the battering and winning and losing, there was still good cheer all around. "At these frolics there was always eating and drinking, it is said, to excess."[71]

One of the oldest and longest running of all Valley contests was the one between the farmers who raised watermelons and boys who stole them. One woman who grew up along Dry River in the late 1800s recalled, "Some years we planted watermelons in a patch west of the barn. Neighborhood boys often stole the melons at night, so we had a shanty to sleep in and keep watch."[72] The best part of a watermelon, it was said, was the stealing.

In a Category by Itself

The Bridgewater *Herald* of July 6, 1903, reported a visit to the town of E. W. Furry of Ft. Worth, Texas, who was a child in Bridgewater in the 1880s. During his visit he noticed the fireflies, and was reminded of a summer pastime that he and his friends thought great "sport" when he was a boy.

How it came about is a mystery, but apparently someone noticed that toads had a voracious appetite for fireflies—they ate all they could hold. Anyway, a few boys got together during the day and rounded up a box full of toads. In the evening they caught fireflies—hundreds of fireflies—and fed them to the toads, who eagerly gobbled them down.

As Mr. Furry recalled, "the old hoppers were so full of the luminous insects that their bodies became transparent. The modern x-ray is a tame affair in comparison." He wondered if Professor Roentgen got the idea for the x-ray "by a toad experiment."

As the boys released their toads on the lawns of old Bridgewater, the effect must have been delightful to behold.[73]

Superstitions, Signs & a Sator

Who hasn't at one time or another called on a superstition in reaction to an unsettling occurrence? Superstitions arrived in the Shenandoah Valley with the early settlers as part of their cultural heritage. The insecurities of day-to-day existence encouraged people to retain them as safeguards against the unknown and unseen, and succeeding generations added to the lore as fancy led them.

Most of us know the dangers of black cats and walking under ladders. These are very common superstitions and will most likely be with us for a long time. Many superstitions have been forgotten, but others are still invoked, although their recognition probably comes from habit rather than belief.

An Old Order Mennonite, when asked about superstitions and why people would put any faith in them, quoted an old Pennsylvania Dutch saying: *"batt's net, schatt's net."*[1] It means "doesn't help, doesn't hurt"—a kind of verbal shrug of the shoulders.[2]

Following are but a sampling of the many forms of superstition to be found in the Valley.

There was a magic spring in the Briery Branch area of Rockingham County. A young woman went there, and with a mirror, looked over her shoulder into the water and saw the image of her future husband reflected on the surface. She recognized him because of a hat he wore all the time.[3]

It's bad luck to lay a hat on the bed.[4]

A cardinal bumping against a window pane is an indication of an impending death.[5] It's also a sign of a coming death if you hear a whacking sound at least three times when you're out in the mountains.[6] In another area it is a sign of death when you hear a ringing in your ears.[7]

In Augusta County it is said to be bad luck if you dream about muddy water.[8] In Rockingham County the superstition is more specific; there they say that to dream of muddy water means a flood is on the way.[9]

An itching nose means a visitor is coming.[10]

Miss Gray Pifer of Mt. Crawford said that if your right eye itches, you will soon be displeased, and if your left eye itches, you will soon be pleased. She also reported that if your right foot itches, you'll soon walk on strange or unfamiliar ground, and if your left foot itches, you'll soon walk in a graveyard.[11]

In eastern Rockingham County it is said to be bad luck to bring a shovel into a house "because it is a grave tool."[12] In Augusta County they don't stop with the shovel but also think a hoe in the house bodes no good.[13]

Peel an apple all in one piece and throw the peel over your shoulder. When you turn around and look at it lying on the ground, whatever letter it reminds you of will be the first letter of your "future husband's last name." When the informant was asked if she had known it to work, she pointed to her husband. "I saw an L," she said, "and there sits Mr. Lam."[14]

In some communities of German ancestry, there was a wedding custom called "Throwing the Stocking." When the newly married couple had been made comfortable in the bridal bed, all the unmarried young people would be admitted to the room. A stocking was rolled into a ball. The young females stood at the foot of the bed, each with her back to the couple. Then each in her turn would throw the stocking over her shoulder and try to hit the bride's head or cap with it; the first to succeed would be the next to marry.[15]

If you are out driving a wagon or buggy and a black cat crosses the road in front of you from right to left, it is a bad sign. If it crosses from the left to the right, there is no reason for concern.[16]

In Augusta County it is thought to be bad luck to point at a rainbow.[17]

It's good luck to scratch your right eye.[18]

Back in the mountains it was said that if someone swept around you, you'd never get married. One woman, however, reported that "they swept around me a lot, but I got married."[19]

It's bad luck to sweep in the house after dark.[20]

If you enter a house in the Valley and leave it without sitting down, it is bad luck.[21] In Rockingham County it is bad luck to enter a house without sitting down if you leave by a different door than the one by which you entered.[22]

Over near Pineville, in Rockingham County, old Arbelia Goodin believed that the ends of her granddaughter's long hair could only be trimmed in the dark of the moon. She took the hair clippings and put them under a rock in a stream.[23] When hair was buried or hidden, it was usually done to insure the child's steady physical growth.

While seated at a table for meals, you might accidently drop one of your eating utensils. If you drop a fork, it means that a man will soon come to the house. If a knife is dropped, a woman will soon appear.[24]

A knife placed under a bed during childbirth will help to relieve the pain.[25]

Old Jim Joseph from near the hamlet of Lilly in Rockingham County used to say that if you dream of a black man and then go hunting up along Blacks Run in the mountains, you'll surely kill a bear.[26]

If a bird flies into your house, there will soon be a death in the family.[27]

Someone in the family will die within six months if a whippoorwill comes to your treetop and sings at night. "In our family it came true."[28]

In Augusta County there is the wonderful saying that if a baby smiles in its sleep, "the child is talking to the angels."[29]

Rain isn't far behind when a tree shows the underside of its leaves.[30]

Along Back Creek in Bath County people used to keep sheep. They grazed them in the mountains both summer and winter. When the sheep came off the mountain to the farmyard gate of their own accord, it was a sure sign of snow. The farmer knew that the snow would soon melt when the sheep became anxious to go back to the mountain.[31]

In Augusta County some people used to count the number of fogs in August. It was thought that there would be exactly that number of snows in the next winter.[32]

Carroll Dennison, a farmer in the Hills of Judea in Augusta County, used to say that if a full moon had a ring around it there would be snow by morning. He also said that if it was a large ring, the number of stars you could count within it would be the number of inches of snow that would fall.[33]

In Rockingham County it is thought that if there is a ring around the moon, the number of stars within it indicates the number of days until a snow or rain will come.[34]

In the Shenandoah Valley, the first sheep shearing of the year usually takes place soon after the first of May. The old timers say that a cold rain will follow within a few days of the shearing—a sheep rain. People used to use the sheep rain as a date to plan other events around. Someone might say, "Let's register that deed at the courthouse before the sheep rain," or "We'll be married after the sheep rain."[35]

In Augusta County a new moon with the points up means dry weather, and a moon with the points down means rain will fall soon.[36] In

Rockingham, shingles put on a roof when the points of the moon are up will cup and leak, and the roof will rot. If it is put on during the time of the moon with points down, the roof will shed water.[37]

"If the sun sets behind a dark cloud, it will rain before morning," say folks in Augusta County.[38]

If it rains on Monday, it will rain two more days that week.[39]

Growing Signs

The astrological sign of Virgo was known to Shenandoah Valley farmers and gardeners as the "Posey Woman."[40] It was also known as the "sign of the flower" in Bath County. Researchers from James Madison University were told by a Back Creek resident that when they planted beans in the sign, "We got blooms; that's all we had."[41] In Augusta County it was considered a barren sign, and it was not considered favorable to plant anything during the period.[42] In the remote area of Criders in Rockingham, it was thought that if you planted in the "Posey Woman" you'd get "more bloom than fruit."[43]

In Bath County, superstitious farmers plant potatoes when the moon is coming up and "growing" full. If this is done, the potatoes will stay near the surface and grow large. Plant when the moon is getting small and the potatoes will grow deep and will not have any size to them.[44] In Augusta County the moon seems to be less of a consideration for planting potatoes. Some folks think that Good Friday is a favorable day to plant the tubers and others (possibly of Irish descent) think Saint Patrick's Day is propitious. You can also plant beans on Good Friday.

Lettuce and peas are best planted on Valentine's Day.[45]

Insuring the flax crop apparently was of great concern to Valley residents. In Augusta County a good growth of flax was promised if you made doughnuts on Shrove Tuesday (the day before Ash Wednesday). In Shenandoah County tangle-cakes (a kind of batter cake made on a griddle) had to be fried up in order for the flax to come in properly.

On Ash Wednesday people in Rockingham County made pancakes or "the chickens wouldn't lay".[46]

Planting by the signs of the Zodiac and on certain days of the calendar was not as widely followed as was planting in the phases of the moon.[47]

Sators

Magic charms, formulas and incantations used by witch doctors to ward off and cure illnesses and hexes were very common in the 18th and 19th centuries; some were used to fulfill wishes and desires. They weren't used exclusively in the Dutch community, but this is where they were the most prevalent.

Perhaps the most famous and most widely used formula was the SATOR. This was a square of letters used to protect buildings from fire. A fire could be extinguished by throwing a plate marked on each side with a SATOR, into a burning structure. The name of God was invoked at the same time as an added measure. It was believed that the fire would die out at once.

It could also protect a person or home from lightning, and it was used as a deterrent to the bewitching of animals, which the people relied on for their livelihood.

The book *Pennsylvania Germans of the Shenandoah Valley* offers this SATOR:

```
S  A  T  O  R
A  R  E  P  O
T  E  N  E  T
O  P  E  R  A
R  O  T  A  S
```

A SATOR from the Timberville area of Rockingham County is a variant of the above and came with instructions as follows:

```
R  O  T  A  S
O  T  E  R  A
T  E  S  E  T
A  R  E  T  O
S  A  T  O  R
```

"The above 25 letteres are correct for anything that is bit by a mad Dog or anything els to be given in there food. to keep them from getting mad. the above was gotten of John Bowman Sen" [sic]

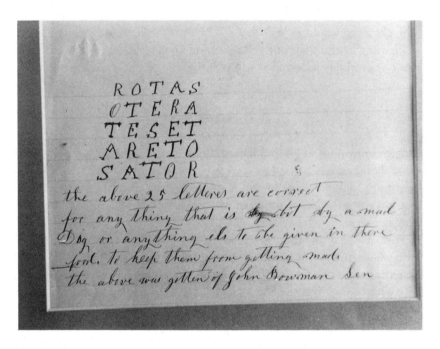

ROTAS
OTERA
TESET
ARETO
SATOR

the above 25 letters are correct
for any thing that is bit by a mad
Dog or anything els to be given in there
food, to keep them from getting made
the above was gotten of John Bowman Sen

A sator: a magic cure for a "mad dog bite."

John Bowman was born in Rockingham County in 1782 and died near Timberville in 1871. This SATOR was found in a group of documents from the M. Otto Zigler estate. All of the papers, some 200 of them, were dated between 1835 and 1863.[48]

Incantations

Most incantations were spoken so as not to be overheard, so not very many survive. The following was written on a slip of paper in Pennsylvania Dutch some time around 1830 in Rockingham County:

Deer Schussbloder (stye on eye)

Schussbloder dud dich oder ich nehm meinen Daumen und dund dich XXX.

It is translated as: stye, do yourself (in) or I'll take my thumb and do you (in).[49] This was remembered by a man who has made a detailed study of the Pennsylvania Dutch.

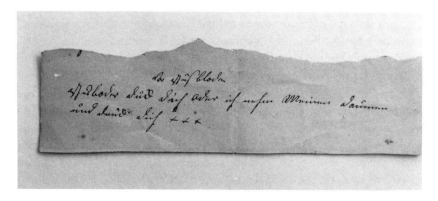

A magic incantation written in Pennsylvania Dutch to "do in" a stye.

To take the fire out of a burn, the following incantation was used in Brocks Gap: *Heili Heili hinckeldreck bis marye iss ales weg*

A loose translation from the Pennsylvania Dutch is: "holy holy chicken manure, by tomorrow morning it will be gone." Possibly chicken manure was used as an ingredient in a poultice to be used on the burn.[50]

A magic incantation to take the fire out of burns was found scribbled on the back of an 1862 Civil War letter in Timberville.

Cure to take out fire
Tree [three] *little ageles* [angels]
came down from
Haven [heaven] *in*
fire & went
Back in frost.[51]

Home Remedies

Charlie Roadcap lived on the western side of Hopkins Gap in Rockingham County, where he did a little farming and chair caning to make a living. He didn't believe in medical doctors and made his own cures from herbs he gathered in the hollows and along the river and in the mountains.

Unlike the other herb doctors of the back country, he only administered to his own family. Some of his cures involved incantations.

When his children came down with deep chest colds, he rubbed goose grease on them. For the croup they were given a tablespoon of rendered fat. One daughter recalled it as "right nasty," and said that her father didn't sugar-coat the taste, though he'd "put a little moonshine in it." She also said that wild honey and rum was used for sinus problems, "and it was good!"

Once, when this daughter cut her leg on a jagged piece of glass, her father made a poultice of cobwebs and leaves and pressed it against the flowing wound. He then said the high words from the Bible for staunching blood. From Ezekiel XVI, 6: "And when I passed by thee, and saw thee polluted in thine own blood, I said unto thee when thou wast in thy blood, Live; yea, I said unto thee when thou wast in thy blood, Live."

And for the distressed Roadcap child, the stream of blood from the injury immediately stopped.[52]

Remedies & Curious Cures

It is difficult at times to distinguish folk remedies from superstitions. Some of the approaches used to cure illnesses in the 19th and early 20th centuries seem absurd to us today, although when they are studied, many prove to have beneficial properties. On the other hand, some methods are found to be detrimental to good health and must be discarded. Some time-honored knowledge has been lost because the country practitioners who used these folk cures were ridiculed by the developing medical profession as being backward and quaint.

With most cures, it helped if the patients believed in the healing power of the herbs, stones, manipulations and incantations or combinations of any of them. Some people living close to the land and the elements had special feelings for the properties of the bounty growing wild in the countryside and the beneficial assocations of living things. Remedies that relied heavily on ritual were probably most successful when taken with an enormous dose of faith.

The herb cures of the folk pharmacopoeia were based in large part on a system of self-reliance that reaches back into pre-history. These treatments were administered by people who studied or had been brought up with the lore. In backcountry cultures, the scarcity of medical doctors and hard currency made the gathering, processing and use of herbs and concoctions important to survival. Even after doctors were common west of the blue mountains, quite a number of people continued to rely on the old ways. Individual farmers, their wives and "granny women" had a tea, poultice or purge for almost every ailment or complaint.

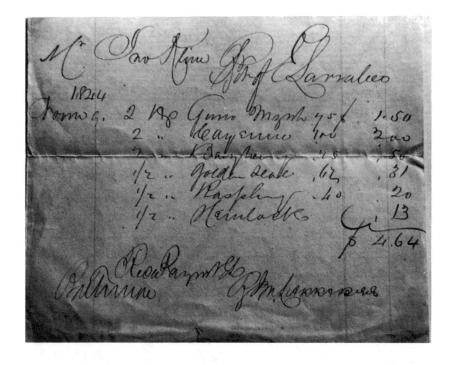

1844 order for herbs by Thomsonian herb doctor John Kline.

The practices became somewhat formalized in the first half of the 19th century. A "doctor" Thomson from New England wrote a book on the uses of herbs in treating illnesses. He licensed practitioners for a nominal fee, sent along his book as a guide, and offered for sale some of the more difficult to find herbs and plant products.[1]

There were a number of Thomsonian herb doctors in the Shenandoah Valley. Two of the most well known were in Rockingham County, both members of pacifist anabaptist religious sects that came to the Valley in the 18th century. Elder John Kline, a Church of the Brethren evangelist, journeyed to remote areas for years bringing the Word of God and physical relief to the afflicted. Kline's treks took him deep into the mountains of what is now West Virginia and into Maryland and Pennsylvania as well. During the Civil War, his comings and goings through federal lines and his willingness to administer treatments to northern as well as southern soldiers led people to suspect him of spying for the North. On June 15, 1864, he was ambushed by several local idlers and killed. He is buried in the Linville Creek Church of the Brethren Cemetery in Broadway, Virginia.

"Doc Gabe" Heatwole, a Mennonite who lived near Mole Hill, was a friend of Kline's. They often went off on herb gathering expeditions together. During Heatwole's long life he not only treated people with herbs but was said to have delivered scores of babies in southwestern Rockingham County. He died on June 18, 1875, well into his 86th year, and is buried in the Shank family cemetery near Dale Enterprise.

The more bizarre cures for disorders thought to be supernatural in nature, cures involving magic, were the specialty of the witch doctors whose powers had been handed down to them by witch doctors of the opposite sex. Seventh sons of seventh sons were thought to have tremendous powers for good and, in some cases, evil. The witch doctor treatments usually involved curious rituals, incantations and sometimes herbs, and were often oriented with the natural elements—phases of the moon, seasons and geological formations.

The following remedies and deterrents to illness are only a few of the hundreds which were known and used by earlier residents of the Shenandoah Valley. These may be among the last folk healing remedies to be collected, as they are quickly fading from memory.

Bark Tea

Old John Croushorn lived with Glenn Wine's family when he was a boy. John was cantankerous and was always picking at young Glenn. Once, when John was down with a cold, he told Glenn to take a hatchet and go out to where an old cherry tree was down and chop him some bark for a tea. He was instructed specifically to chop in the direction of the top of the tree. If he were to chop downward, he was told, the resulting brew would drive the cold down into Mr. Croushorn's lungs. Glenn said he chopped the bark "down," but old John eventually got well anyway.[2]

A Clarke County informant reported, "Daddy used wild cherry bark for colds. Skinned the outside bark away and used the middle bark to boil for a tea."[3]

Another informant, from Rockingham County, says to scrape the inner bark of the wild cherry tree; boil it down to a syrup for coughs.[4] (Now we've covered all of the layers of cherry tree bark.)

A Speedy and Permanent Cure

A printed recipe for "the Speedy and Permanent Cure of Consumption, Asthma, Catarrh, Bronchitis, and all Throat and Lung Affections" was making the rounds in Shenandoah County in the late 19th century as it doubtlessly was elsewhere in the Valley and the United States. A "doctor," W. W. Sherar of New York, sent it out free of charge as his contribution to the well being of mankind. He called his cure *Cannabis Sativa*. Supposedly the recipe was given to him by a missionary, who had gotten it from native "Medicine Men" of India.

The ingredients for this magical syrup are enough to take anyone's mind off their ills. They include:

Extract Asiatic Cannabis Sativa—Two Ounces
Extract Asiatic Halish Sativa—Three Ounces
Verbena Hastata—Two Drochms
Extract Diosma—Three Drochms
Pulv. Cinchoni Bark—Two Ounces
Ext. Cashgar Leaves (Blood Root)—Three Ounces
Inulin—Three Ounces
Loaf Sugar—One Pound
Rum or Gin—Half Pint
Cold Water—One Pint

All of the above "extracts and powdered roots, barks and herbs" were to be thoroughly compounded and mixed together and put in a bottle holding at least three pints. To this would be added one half pint of warm water, it would be shaken vigorously, then left to stand for ten minutes. Next, a pint of water with a pound of sugar dissolved in it was to be added, and after that the half pint of "Rum or Holland Gin" was to be poured in. Again it was to be well shaken, then left to sit until cold. And then, said the directions, "you have a beautiful Syrup ready to use."

"Doctor" Sherar, after volumes of descriptions of his syrup's curative powers, finally mentioned that it rarely takes more than two boxes to effect a lasting cure. The "two boxes" leads one to suspect that "Doctor" Sherar's intentions weren't quite altruistic; try finding Extract Asiatic Halish Sativa (a mixture of hashish and opium) in downtown Toms Brook.[5]

Asafetida

Asafetida is a relative of the parsley family and produces a gum resin. It is very pungent. Inch or inch-and-a-half square bags of asafetida were worn on a string around the necks of children as a deterrent to sinus problems. In Hopkins Gap, asafetida was thought to be of use in repelling witches.[6] One woman, when remembering children wearing the bags, exclaimed, "Oh, they smelled!"[7]

Dr. M. Ellsworth Kyger of Bridgewater is an acknowledged expert on the dialects that have been grouped under the language heading of Pennsylvania Dutch, a combination of English and German. According to Dr. Kyger, people living in the Shenandoah Valley who were of Pennsylvania-Dutch ancestry referred to asafetida as *Deivelsdreck,* which translates to devil's dirt or dung. In medieval Germany it was called *Teufelsdreck,* which also means devil's dung.

Arbelia Morris Goodin lived with her son's family near Pineville in Rockingham County. She was from Bacon Hollow, on the east side of the Blue Ridge. When her sister came to visit she'd bring asafetida and other herbs from the hollow. She also brought over a little "toddy" (moonshine). Arbelia would dose her grandchildren when they were sick and made them wear the asafetida; it kept everything "from witches to mice" away.[8]

A surviving account book (1804 to 1825) from the Michael Baker Store in Brocks Gap in northwestern Rockingham County shows that the use of asafetida was general enough

Arbelia Goodin, "granny woman" of Bacon Hollow and Pineville.

so that it was stocked for sale in back country stores. In March of 1804 Baker sold one ounce of "asifidity" to Peter Wezel for 1 shilling 6 pence. Several other families purchased the herbal concoction during the same period.[9]

As late as the early 1970s, a pharmacy in Staunton continued to stock little squares of asafetida because it was still called for occasionally.[10]

Warts

Many wart remedies seem to share a common theme of transference, but the interpretations vary widely, as reports of these "wart doctors" show.

Bill Flemings, when hired to remove a person's warts, would spit tobacco juice on the growth, tie a string around it and say some magic words. If the person refused the tobacco juice, Bill would tell them with some irritation to go find some milkweed. He'd squeeze the plant's juice on the wart and then mutter his incantation.[11]

Arbelia Goodin cured warts by scrubbing the warts on the hand briskly with bean leaves. While she did this she whispered incantations under her breath.[12]

Aunt Eliza Kyger, who lived in the Mill Creek area of Rockingham County, was a renowned wart doctor, but her husband, Frank, was a non-believer in the wart removal rituals practiced by his wife. Once, while she was away from home, a little boy came by to seek her services. He was crestfallen when Frank told him of her absence. Frank told the boy not to worry, that he'd remove the wart. He waved his hands over the wart, uttered some made up mumbo-jumbo, and told the boy to go home, that the wart would soon disappear. Several weeks later the boy returned with his little brother, who had warts needing to be cured. He didn't want to see Aunt Eliza though, he wanted Uncle Frank.[13]

Aunt Annie Laura Gordon who lived on North River in Rockingham County cured warts by rubbing fat meat on them. The fat meat was then wrapped in a white cloth and buried under a downspout.[14]

Rebecca Jane Kiracofe (1867-1950) and her grandchildren. She was a "granny woman" of the village of Sangerville.

Rebecca Jane Kiracofe was a herb doctor who lived at Sangerville in Augusta County. She also "removed" warts. One of her methods was to rub a bean on the patient's wart, wrap the bean in brown paper tied up with string and have the person put it under a downspout at their home. Rebecca Jane would also give a child a penny for a wart.[15]

Grover Moyers attended a district church meeting in Rockingham County's Brocks Gap Region around 1900. A man he did not know noticed a wart on Grover's hand. The stranger said, "See me after the meeting and I'll take that wart off for you." When the meeting broke up for the day, the two men got together. The wart doctor took out a ten-penny nail and touched the head of it to Grover's wart while mumbling some magic words. Grover was told that the wart would be gone in two weeks—and it was.[16]

There were also do-it-yourself wart cures. One wart remedy from Rockbridge County directs the sufferer to steal a neighbor's washcloth, rub his wart with it and then bury it. When the cloth rots, the wart will be gone. Another Rockbridge remedy involves cutting an onion into four pieces. The wart is pricked until it bleeds, then each quarter of the onion is touched to the wart. Finally, the pieces are buried in the "dreep" (drip) of the roof. When it rains again, the wart will be gone. "Dreep" is a Scots-Irish word; a good portion of the people of Rockbridge County are of that descent.[17]

🍁

Or if all that fails, here are three more self-cures for warts:

> To get rid of warts tie a knot in a string for each wart you have and bury it under a rock. When the string rots, the warts will be gone.[18]

> Pick up a bone and rub it on your wart if you want to get rid of it. You have to lay the bone down in the same position it was in when you picked it up. The wart will soon disappear.[19]

> Make a notch in a twig for each wart you want to get rid of. Wrap up the twig in pretty paper with a bow, like a gift, and leave it on a path that other children travel. When it is picked up, the warts will go away. The unfortunate child who picked it up gets the warts.[20]

Madstones

Perhaps the rarest of all the strange cures in Virginia are the madstones. They were variously described as having been formed in the stomachs of deer or made of a compound in the Orient and sold as "snake stones" to seafarers, who brought them back to America. They were known and used as early as the 18th century east of the mountains.

These small, hard objects were said to have the power to draw poison from the bite of a snake or a rabid animal or insect. Some stones were so revered that shares were sold in them so that they would be available to more people when an urgent need arose.

There are many sworn accounts of madstones being placed on wounds and adhering without being bound in place. They stuck tight for a matter of minutes, hours or days, falling off only when they had absorbed all of the poison. Some madstones were soaked in water after their use, and green fluid was observed leaking from them.

At various times there were said to be madstones in circulation in Shenandoah, Frederick and Clarke Counties.[21]

Remedy Against the Mad Dog Bite

Some herb doctors were good businesspeople. They had printed instructions for the cure of various maladies. These were sold for a few coins to people who lived in the backcountry, to be used when needed. One that has survived comes from Timberville, in Rockingham County. It is printed in "Pennsylvania Dutch" and has several blanks to be filled in, making it possible to tailor the cure to the specific purchaser. This is the translation:

> Take a hand full of dried *red chickweed* pour two quarts of good beer over it and cook it in a new covered earthenware pot until half of it is cooked down. It must be cooked over a gentle fire. The pot in which it is cooked must be kept totally clean and not used for anything else. When the herb is cooked enough, and stirred, and then pressed well through a clean cloth so that all the residue is removed. Then add to the potion two drams of the best *Venecian Theriack* (another herb).
>
> It has to dissolve and be mixed thoroughly. For a fasting man or a head of cattle give them the following portions in the morning. For a strong healthy man a pint all at once if possible, if not then in smaller doses. If taken all at once, this is better. If there are signs of madness, the medicine should be repeated for two or three mornings. Should there be real signs of madness then you should give larger doses of the herbs in the above named quantity of beer. A woman should take less than a man approximately a third or a half as much. The amount for a child should be determined by its age and constitution. It should be noted that children according to their age can tolerate more of the medicine in proportion to adults. The mother or person nursing a baby should take an extra

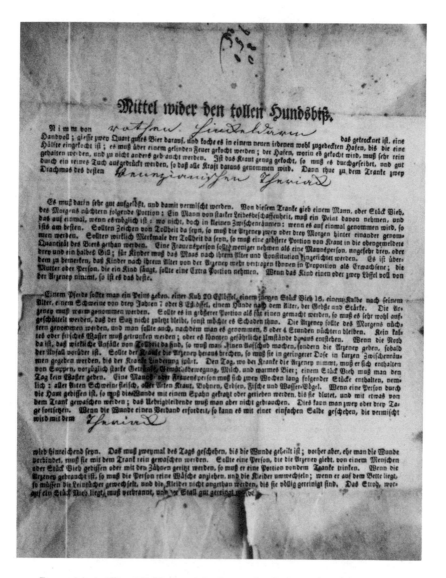

Pennsylvania "Dutch" (German) herb cure for the bite of a mad dog, with additional ingredients handwritten in the blank spaces.

dose. It is best if the child takes one or two teaspoons of the medicine.

Give a horse a pint, a cow 20 tablespoons, young cattle 16, a calf according to age, a pig of three years of age 7 or 8 tablespoons, a dog according to its age and strength.

The medicine must be warm when taken. Take it in morning on an empty stomach and don't eat for three or four hours afterwards. Do not drink any cold or fresh water; this could cause dangerous effects. Hold back the medicine if there is a real attack of madness, then resume as soon as the fits subside. If the patient throws up then give smaller doses in shorter time frames until the patient's problems are alleviated. On the day the patient takes the medicine he must abstain from soups, especially strong drinks, vegetables, milk and warm beer. Cannot give cattle any water. A man or woman must, for two weeks, not eat any kind of pork, all forms of cabbage, beans, peas, fish and water fowl. If the bite pierced the skin of a person, then the wound must be pinched until it bleeds and then washed with the potion solution. If the wound needs to be bandaged then put a simple salve which is mixed with the *Theriack* on it. This has to be done twice a day until the wound is healed. However, before you bandage the wound, the wound should be washed clean with the potion. Should the person administering the medicine be bitten by either the (human) patient or the head of cattle he (or she) must also drink a dose of the potion. In handling the medicine the person must have on clean clothes. When the patient is in bed then the bed linens must be changed and the clothing not worn again until thoroughly clean. In the stable the straw must be burned and the stall thoroughly cleaned.[22]

More Curious Cures

Horse chestnuts carried in a pocket are thought to ward off rheumatism.[23]

Snake root tea is good for "high blood" (pressure).[24]

"Sassafras tea is good to thin blood."[25]

A tea or broth made from the hind legs of mice is used for kidney ailments.[26]

Children with whooping cough in the Centerville area of Augusta County were passed through a horse collar as a cure.[27]

For someone who is weak and recovering from a prolonged illness, make them a broth from sparrows. They'll get their strength back quickly.[28]

In the Hopkins Gap region of Rockingham County, rendered skunk fat was used to grease the chest for croup. The informant also stated that "a half a teaspoon is also taken inward for croup."[29]

If you have chapped lips, you can get relief by kissing the middle rail in a five-rail fence.[30]

When Rebecca Jane Michael heard that neighbors were planning to take their new baby out for a ride for the first time, she showed up at their door with an old, cracked saucer containing hard bear grease. She put it on the stove to warm, and when it softened, she rubbed a little on one of the baby's palms and on the bottom of the opposite foot. It was thought that a baby's first outing would result in a sore and cranky baby, but greasing by the herb lady would protect the baby from the rigors of the journey.[31]

At Pineville, in Rockingham County, they believed that if you wrapped a stocking around a sore throat, it would soon be cured.

In the same area it was thought that if a person who never knew his father blew into the face of a person suffering with mumps, they would be easier to endure and would soon disappear.[32]

A buzzard's feather stuck in a hat will help to relieve rheumatism.[33]

Carry a hog's tooth in your right pocket if you want to ward off a toothache. This must be for luck—who ever heard of a hog with a toothache![34]

According to the Lexington *Gazette*, in 1835 the Harper and Moore Store in Collierstown had "the original receipt for Lehman's Celebrated Worm Tea."[35] Whether the concoction was made from worms or was used to cure people or animals with worms was not explained; in that period it could very well have been either.

For a sprained ankle take catnip, sprinkle salt on it and bind it to the ankle.[36] "Mullin Tea" was also used for sprained ankles. The leaves of the mullein plant were boiled in vinegar and water and the ankle was bathed in it while it was still warm. The informant observed, "Don't see it [the plant] about much any more."[37]

Catnip tea was made for children with the colic.[38]

"Most people in our section would rub turpentine on a sprain. You never covered it or it would burn."[39]

Queen Anne's Lace made into a tea is said to relieve backache.[40]

Sage and honey tea is a good brew to give to someone with pneumonia.[41]

Lobelia tea was used by Thomsonian herb doctor Gabe Heatwole as a purge.[42] Lobelia is an annual or perennial plant of the bellflower family.

Drinking tea made from the aromatic sage is said to keep a woman's hair from turning grey prematurely.[43]

In some areas a three-colored cat was thought to prevent convulsions in children. A three-year-old child who had convulsions was given such a kitten to play with. The two were inseparable, and soon the convulsions disappeared forever from the child. When the cat was half grown, it began to have convulsions.[44]

Goldenseal and Comfort Root teas are good for an upset stomach.[45]

If you have kidney problems, swamp root tea can be used for relief.[46]

"One time the family was down with measles. I put sheep manure in boiling water, strained it, and added two ounces of moonshine. It wasn't long before those measles started popping out."[47]

Undergrown children in the Runions Creek section of Brocks Gap in Rockingham County were measured with a string made by a young girl on a spinning wheel. After the measuring, the string was buried. When it began to rot, the child would begin to grow normally.[48]

"Greasy Mustard" plaster was used on the sufferer's chest for a deep cold. Many informants spoke of being burned by mustard plasters, but this one was made with lard and spread on a cloth that could be placed on the patient without burning.[49] Another non-burning plaster was made with mustard, lard and egg whites.[50]

A family in Singer Glen used a mustard and lard poultice for pneumonia. When the patient's chest started to turn red, it was removed. The patient was washed off thoroughly, and then a hot onion poultice was applied.

"For a bad cold or pleurisy, they'd put lard on your chest with salt sprinkled on it of a night."[51]

Ginseng, a man-shaped root, wasn't used as a treatment by most Shenandoah Valley residents and gatherers. It was a mountain cash crop along with hides and tanning bark and was sold or traded for use elsewhere. The root was dried and sold by the pound, usually ending up in the Orient, where it was used for many purposes including as an aphrodisiac.[52] The gathering of ginseng continues today.

Acute cases of poison ivy and poison oak have often been treated at

Seawright Springs in Augusta County. It is said that the cure involves bathing in the ice-cold waters of the runoff stream; this alone takes great fortitude. Upon leaving the healing waters, the patient must rub the tender water plants which grow there on the afflicted area and leave them to dry. By the next day a cure will have been accomplished.[53]

A tea made from peppermint leaves will stop a stomachache.[54]

Freckles can be washed away on the first of May. If they are washed in morning dew, they will be transferred to the hands, which can be dried on another part of the body—like the arms or legs or an area that isn't normally seen. The freckles will be transferred to that place permanently. Some people in Augusta County thought that this had to be repeated three years in a row to work.[55]

When mumps invaded the home, it was traditional to put hog manure on the throat as a relief or cure.[56]

Pennyroyal tea was used to break a fever, for upset stomach and to treat the common cold.[57] It is of the same family as mint and yields an aromatic oil.

Near Timberville, in Rockingham County, the people had a novel way of curing children of chronic asthma or croup. The child was taken to the woods, where the father drilled a hole in a tree with an auger. A lock of the child's hair was put in the hole, and the hole was plugged up. This was considered a sure cure.[58]

Goiters, large growths on the neck caused by an inflammation of the thyroid, were treated mostly by Brauche, a special healing power possessed by only a few people. Near the village of Spring Creek, in Rockingham County, goiters were removed in the dark of the moon. Words from the Bible were said three times as hands were rubbed over the growth. "My mother's sister used to take off goiters for people. She did it in the dark of the moon. My husband here had an inward goiter she cured for him. She said words from the Bible, but she couldn't tell me because if she did, she'd lose her charm. She rubbed her hands over it, too, and said the words three times."[59]

Thrash or thrush, open sores in the mouth, was cured with a straw ritual with several variants. One was to go to the stable and remove straw from horse manure. It would be drawn through the mouth of the sufferer three times while a powerful incantation was uttered; it was supposed to be from the Bible. The practitioner said the "high words," then tied a string around the straws and hung them "in back of the stove or next to the chimney." The thrash would disappear when the straw dried out.[60]

A woman witch doctor was called to a home near Mole Hill in Rockingham County in 1912 to cure a sick child. The informant, who witnessed the cure, told us, "In our family we had a baby sick with the thrash and an old woman—old to me: I was six—was called in to cure." Her name was Heatwole, and she used straw, as others did, to treat this ailment. She drew it through the baby's mouth and said some words softly, so no one could hear. Then she left, taking the straw with her. The informant said that the child was cured, but it didn't seem to happen any sooner than it normally would have.[61]

During the Civil War, some Valley soldiers chewed dried slippery elm bark when in battle or on the march. It was said to relieve thirst and hunger.[62]

When on the march, Valley soldiers of German ancestry stopped at farms where they knew German people lived. They'd fill up mess kits with sauerkraut, thus helping themselves to avoid colds and like illnesses that invaded the camps.[63]

From Page County comes a handwritten "Receipt for Curing pains" circa 1860: "Take a quart Alcahol 4 ounces Camphire 3 table spoons of Mustard 9d worth cayan peper 4 lbs worth Docters casteel soap a little harts horn and Laudnum all put together and boilt a short time."[64]

In Page County a woman said that her grandfather smoked a corncob pipe, and if a child in the family had an earache, he'd blow smoke in the ear as a cure. She also said that for a spider bite, you should cut a piece from a new potato and hold it against the bite. Eventually the potato will turn black as it absorbs the venom.

Miss Gray Pifer of Mt. Crawford said that "horehound grew down near the creek. Momma made a horehound syrup with brown sugar for coughs."

Witches & Witch Doctors

Witches

Witches have not been tried, jailed or executed in America since the early 18th century, but tales of their activities persist. During that period in our history, superstitious practices invoked for self-protection were considered as prudent dabbling in the occult and virtually harmless. Powers or practices called upon for mean-spirited or evil purposes, however, were considered to be witchcraft, and mysterious negative occurrences were attributed to malevolent people in the community who wielded demonic powers. Despite the perception of evil, people suspected of being witches, who were mostly women, were often tolerated in society because of their family ties or from a fear of retribution—no one wanted to get on the wrong side of a witch.

According to the social standards of the day, women on all levels of society were supposed to guide the domestic household and to provide light conversation for the world-weary and hard-working menfolk at the end of the day. If she were independent and outspoken, or inclined to show off her intelligence, she was liable to be the topic of whispered conversations among both sexes. Such non-traditional behavior was seen as a threat to the male oligarchy and was a mystery to the other females. The woman might at first be called a witch simply as a derogatory comment on her non-conformist behavior, but let that word be uttered often enough and imaginations would tag her with more sinister crimes against peace and harmony.

Two cases in point were a certain Mrs. Hagerty and Mary McDowell Greenlee, both of Augusta County. Mrs. Hagerty, who was born in

Ireland, was a poor widow who lived in the county seat of Staunton. Beside the misfortune of being left alone to provide for her young children, she had suffered a grievous accident that left the lower portion of her face scarred and terribly burnt. She wore a scarlet cloth to hide this disfigurement, which left only her bright and intelligent eyes showing—enough to start a rumor that his strange woman was a witch.

Her small hovel was near the Episcopal burying ground on Spring Alley, and people said that Beelzebub visited her nightly while making his rounds through the old cemetery. She was described as "lean and bony" and her children as "half starved." That she kept a fat black cat amid these scenes of poverty certainly added to the notion that she was a communicant of the devil. People so feared passing Mrs. Hagerty's house that luxuriant grass grew in the seldom-used lane that ran in front of it.

As an interesting aside, her son, James Hagerty, was taken under the wing of one of Staunton's leading merchants, Robert Gamble. James took well to business and soon traveled back and forth to England, where he represented Mr. Gamble's interests with Liverpool merchants. In time he opened his own firm in that city, dealing in American cotton and tobacco, and became a merchant prince there. At the time of his death in the mid-1840s, he was the United States consul in Liverpool.

Mary McDowell Greenlee was a member of one of the early landed gentry families of Augusta County. Like Mrs. Hagerty, she was widowed when young, but unlike most women of her social position, she did not choose to remarry and join her holdings with those of a new husband. Instead, she showed a pronounced independent streak and vowed that she would manage her own affairs. Her lifestyle, and her way of putting herself on the same plane in business matters as the men, set tongues to wagging, and rumors that she must be in league with Satan spread.

It is doubtful that anything concerning her being a suspected witch was ever said to her face, but through the years she felt the tension in the air, and she played to it. Because she was a member of one of the leading families, she was not ostracized and entertained guests in her home on various social occasions. Once, while hosting a quilting party and making every effort to be hospitable, she pressed one of the industrious ladies to eat more with the words, "The mare that does double work should be best fed." Those teasing words set off wild speculation in the community—witches were said to turn victims into horses and ride them through the night, returning them exhausted to their true form at the approach of dawn suffering with intense fatigue but no memory of the occurrence.

Missing livestock in the area was put down to one of her spells, and it was said that she would "go forth into the open air" at night and utter "incantation and curses," which made her neighbors shrink from her. It must also be said that she was noted for her "vivacity and intellect," which was often cancelled by her "eccentricities of character and conduct."

She was an aunt of one of the early governors of the commonwealth, James McDowell of Rockbridge County. When she was past four score and ten, she testified at length in hearings concerning pre-Revolutionary War land holdings and boundaries in the upper Shenandoah Valley. Her memory was so keen that she was never questioned as to accuracy.[1]

Witch Doctors

Witch doctors, mostly men, were consulted to counteract certain activities of witches. They were held in high regard, and their names were rarely spoken, in order to protect them from the evil machinations of those who practiced the dark arts. One informant, when asked if he had ever known a witch doctor, answered without hesitation in the affirmative. His wife, who was in the room at the time, exclaimed, "You did? You never told me!"

Granny Fawley (1842-1925)

The informant had been delivered at his birth near the end of the 19th century by Granny Fawley, a midwife and witch doctor in the Genoa area of Brocks Gap. When children came down with a mysterious illness and everyone suspected witches of preying on the innocent, she was called in to effect a cure.[2]

Granny, whose real name was Sarah Fulk Fawley, was also called Sarah "Mam."[3] She "grannied" over a wide area, usually traveling by horseback accompanied only by her foster son, Laney Custer, when he was young. She more than earned the title of "Granny" in the years she served as a midwife. In one family alone, that of Abe Carr, she delivered all fourteen children.[4]

She treated babies for thrash or thrush in the role of a witch doctor with a ritual involving magic incantations.[5]

She was remembered as "a kindhearted woman who never turned away from her door anyone who was in need," and her obituary called her "the Brocks Gap Angel of Mercy."[6]

The concern over the welfare of children is a common thread in stories about the spells of witches being treated by the good powers of witch doctors.

An artist's impression of Aunt Vic Keller.

Uncle Sam and Aunt Vic Keller were former slaves who lived near Staunton at the end of the 19th century. Aunt Vic was greatly respected and sought after as a healer. She especially cared for children, and she was often consulted in cases where regular medical doctors were baffled. Illnesses that couldn't be explained by science were thought supernatural in origin by some people.[7]

On January 31, 1919, the people of Rockingham County living in the North River basin read in the Harrisonburg newspaper the bizarre account of what must have seemed an invasion of witches—very strange things were occurring on a farm two miles northeast of Mt. Crawford. In the florid style common to the times, it was related that the home of W. H. Ponton was "infested with witches, who are most mischievous in their manner, and daring in their deeds."

Many witch doctors were consulted, but to no avail. Some of them concluded that, "Beelzebub is forming the nucleus of a vast army of evil spirits ... with the intention of invading the habitats of all the county's citizens." The witches were not accused of any deeds that resulted in tragedy, but some of the manifestations were definitely of a dangerous nature. Butcher knives were said to fly through the air, and pies baking in the stove mysteriously fell out onto the floor. Buckets of freshly drawn water tasted as if someone had poured soap into them.

One of the women of the household saw the apparition of a man with an apron tied around him when she went to the cellar for something; it quickly melted away. Mr. Ponton went to the barn at dusk one evening and saw a woman appear, leave the barn silently, and then vanish into the night. Cows would not go near the barn, and horses there kept breaking their tethers in fear of something unseen by the people.

The mayor of Mt. Crawford, O. A. Layman, was called in, but he said that he witnessed nothing. Another witch doctor of the neighborhood was consulted, and he reported that there were seven witches in the immediate area, that the one doing the "mysterious tricks" was the fourth of the group, and that she traveled "on the wind at the proper hour of night."[8]

More Than Human

There was an old Pennsylvania Dutch saying that was used when speaking of someone who was thought to be involved in the dark arts. The old timers would say that he or she "could do more than eat bread;" which must have meant that the person was taking part in something beyond the daily existence known to most people.[9]

Precautions

Certain precautions could be taken to protect yourself, your property and your family from the mischief of witches. Near the village of Jerome, in Shenandoah County, it was said that some people plugged up their keyholes to keep witches from entering their houses.[10]

In Augusta County, in the Naked Creek region, there was a woman who believed in being prepared. Catherine Wine wasn't sure she knew any witches personally, but her farm was in the Hills of Judea, a rather isolated area, and being a practical "Dutch" lady, she thought it best to be safe. Her husband Samuel often chided her for her superstitions, especially when they concerned his barn. When Catherine was growing up, there was a great fear of witches getting into the barn on Halloween and vexing the animals, so to ward off trouble, Catherine greased the corners of the barn every year when that evening came around. Apparently the witches were supposed to enter the structure at the corners, and the grease made them slide off when they made the attempt.

Catherine was also concerned about her butter. She strongly suspected that witches would not miss an opportunity to hex her churn and prevent the butter from firming up. To counter this, she put needles in the churn before she began to make the butter. She and her little granddaughter, Annie Hill, counted them as they were dropped into the cream and counted them again when they paddled the butter out of the churn and into the firkins.

Catherine wasn't the only Valley housewife who protected her butter. In Highland County, near Doe Hill, the same problem was addressed by putting a hot iron wedge into the churn.[11]

Near Broadway, in Rockingham County, the cream was poured into a trough and whipped vigorously. It was thought that as the butter was formed, the witch who had hexed it was also whipped. Silver coins were put in churns around Moscow, in Augusta County, to thwart the doings of witches.[12]

When a rifle wouldn't shoot straight, this problem was often attributed to a hex. Some early gunsmiths used the stratagem of engraving a circular design, called a "witches' ring," around the bore opening of the rifle. Rifles that weren't protected with the ring could be put in jeopardy if their owners crossed someone who could loose evil upon them.

A witch doctor could remove a spell from a rifle or, if you lived in Augusta County or southern Rockingham County, you could have taken care of matters yourself at Clamper Spring in the Hills of Judea. It was believed that the spring had magical properties, and that tow, the fiber of flax or jute, that was wrapped around the end of the ramrod, dipped into the water, and then used to wipe out the barrel, would immediately remove the hex and protect the rifle forever.[13]

Hoodoo Spring

Down the road from Catherine Wine's place was Seawright Springs. Slaves in the area called it Hoodoo Spring and believed that it was a gathering place for witches. More specifically, they believed that every

Friday night, at one o'clock, the witches danced around the pool. They said that barrels rolled down to the spring from an old burying ground on a hill to the east when the witches danced, and as the barrels neared the circle of dancing witches, they became phosphorescent, and headless men and women emerged and joined the dance.

Legend also tells us that anyone brave enough to bathe in the spring while the dance is in progress would become immortal. The first person to drink from the water the next morning would be given the gift of a long life and the ability to foresee the future. The first person to bathe in the spring following the dance would "never have sickness or sorrow."[14]

Witches of Rockingham County

There are traditions of several witches in the Brocks Gap area of Rockingham County in the late 19th and early 20th centuries.

Catherine Dove was always referred to as "Kate the Witch." Once, when she went to visit the home of her neighbor, Paul Smith, a broom had fallen and lay across the threshold. She would not enter the house until someone picked up the broom.[15] This strengthened her reputation as a witch, as it is well known that a witch cannot step over a broom.

Up in the Gap, on the northwestern border of Rockingham County and Hardy County, West Virginia, there lived a husband and wife by the name of Halterman. They didn't get along with each other very well. Mr. Halterman sometimes drank moonshine to excess, and this put his wife into a black mood. Her anger was to be feared, because she was a witch.

Mr. Halterman could not resist the jug, even though he knew that he would have to face Mrs. Halterman's peculiar method of punishment. The next day, from sunrise to sunset, he would be followed by big black bears and tawny mountain lions as he did his chores around the farm. They never attacked him, but they were unsettling nonetheless as they crept about and watched his every move.[16]

A young man named Reuben Dove courted one of the Feaster sisters; it was brave of him, since it was rumored that she was a witch. He visited her one winter evening, and after awhile decided he should start for home. She insisted that he stay, but he said that he "was boss" and was leaving. She said, "You'll see something."

As he approached the bridge at the river, something stepped out from behind an oak tree and pushed him into the icy water. By the time he got home, his clothes were frozen stiff. The next day he returned to the spot.

There had been snow on the ground for several days, and no new snow had fallen. The only tracks near or around the tree were his own. He soon turned his attentions to another girl in the district.[17]

There was a witch who lived along Redbank Run in southwestern Rockingham County; her name was Melinda Knisley. She lived at the end of a long lane, with her husband, Peter, in the shadow of the mountains. Peter worked on and off as a farmhand and cut a little firewood to sell now and then. In reality, neither of them were known to work very hard.

Just down the road from Melinda's place was the home of Martha Ellen Wheelbarger. Early one day Melinda visited Martha Ellen, and while there she noticed a basket of sweet potatoes up on top of the pie safe. Melinda said that she wanted them for the hot-bed she was already preparing in her garden. Martha Ellen refused the request, and Melinda went away in an ill humor. Martha Ellen hoped that was the end to the matter, but she worried anyway; it was dangerous to offend a witch.

A few hours later she saw Melinda coming back down the road, and something in her demeanor alerted Martha Ellen to potential trouble. Thinking quickly, Martha Ellen dropped a broom on the floor across her open doorway. Melinda came up on the porch, stood there with her hands on her hips, and in no uncertain terms demanded that the sweet potatoes be handed over to her. She chanced to look down and saw the broom. "Why, Ellie," she said in a quiet, admonishing tone, "you're awfully careless with that broom." She then turned sharply on her heel and walked away.

Mrs. Fannie Pence and her family lived up near the head spring of Beaver Creek. There came a day when Melinda was out and about, seeing what she could borrow or beg from her neighbors, and at Mrs. Pence's, she begged specifically for fresh milk, but there was none to spare. This made Melinda very angry, but she went away. Later on Melinda's husband showed up, and he also begged for some milk, with the same result.

That night the Pence's baby daughter became ill and wouldn't stop crying. The Pences were worried that Melinda had put a spell on the child in revenge for having been refused the milk earlier in the day. The next morning they consulted a local "white" witch doctor, who said he believed that a witch had truly bedeviled the infant. He sold the Pences a charm, and the baby was soon restored to normal. Later they heard that Melinda had suddenly and inexplicably begun to cry at about the time their baby had stopped wailing.

Hensel and Lizzie Croushorn lived on the road going up to Union Springs. They had two fine work horses that they fairly doted on. It was not surprising that they became greatly alarmed when both horses came down with a mysterious illness. They had never seen anything like it and almost immediately began to suspect that the witch, Melinda, had put a hex on their horses.

The Croushorns visited a fortune teller, who told Mrs. Croushorn that the spell could be removed if she would build a fresh fire in her stove and keep poking it with a flesh fork until it burned down to embers. She went home and did as she was instructed.

Over on Redbank Run Melinda suddenly complained to Peter that she felt prickly all over. The curse was broken and the horses were restored to health.[18]

Eliza Croushorn wanted to identify a witch in her neighborhood just west of Clover Hill. When she saw the woman she suspected coming up the path toward her house, she threw the broom down across the open doorway. The old woman came onto the porch as if to enter but brought herself up short when she saw the broom lying there.

"Aunt Eliza," she said sweetly, "I see your broom's fell down. I'll pick it up." And she did so before going in, leaving Eliza to still wonder.[19]

Since Melinda Knisley would not pick up a broom, this must have been a different woman from the same area.

In the Eye of the Beholder

Witches have been described in many different ways; how they are perceived varies from one culture to another. Because the Shenandoah Valley was settled by people from northern Europe and the British Isles, we have several views of them. Ill-natured old women were looked upon with circumspection. Some were represented as being crones, while others were remembered as "sensitive and fragile of body." With the aid of a witch's brew made up of certain herbs, they could make themselves seem beautiful in the eyes of men and wildly desirable.[20]

To be sure, some individuals who were thought to be practitioners of unholy rites were young and did not fit the common image of a witch. Ivy Lamb was not one of these. She lived by Hoover's Bridge near Brocks Gap, and everyone in the neighborhood thought that she must be a witch. Her long, stringy hair, grey clothing and big, black shoes undoubtedly contributed to the suspicion.

Ivy shared her house with a score of cats, and she had chairs for each of them to curl up in. When she had a visitor, she would address one of the cats by name and say, "George, now get down off the chair, for we have company." The named cat would obey.

What most reinforced the suspicion that she was a witch were her pet snakes, who shared the house with her and the cats. Some of them lived up the chimney and others called the dresser drawers home. Sometimes, when she was talking to a guest or one of the cats, she'd turn toward the hearth or the bureau and say to the reptiles, "Now, I don't want you to think that I'm ignoring you."[21]

In the Saumsville area of Shenandoah County there was a house that had a hole drilled in the doorsill. An oxen's tail stood up in the hole to ward off witches. It was thought to be an old world custom brought to the Valley by the Pennsylvania-Germans.[22]

Out of Retirement

In the Bennetts Run region of Brocks Gap, it was rumored that in her younger days old Mattie had practiced witchcraft. If you crossed Mattie back then, it was said, you risked a hex on your cows that made them give bloody milk. Maybe it *was* just a rumor, but it was an unsettling thought all the same. Mattie's husband died in the late 1930s, and, as was the custom, the neighbors came by to keep vigil with the new widow. They sat quietly for a time, Mattie rocking and smoking her corncob pipe, then she broke the silence with a chilling statement: "Now that Pap's dead, I guess I'll go back to witchin'." All of the visitors made "an immediate exit!"[23]

Sorcerers

There were a few men who were masters of dark powers; they were called sorcerers. They were rarely spoken of, and although the feeling conveyed in these stories is that witches on the whole were considered merely a nuisance, there was genuine fear that if sorcerers were stirred up, the consequences could be unspeakable. One informant alluded to a witch doctor who had given himself over to evil. Even though the alleged sorcerer must have been dead for many years, the informant would not speak his name.[24]

The belief in witches has all but left the Valley, though it is likely that in some remote hollows of West Virginia, loneliness, isolation and fear of the unknown can still summon them up in the minds of the people.

The Supernatural

People telling stories about ghosts or other strange manifestations usually preface their tales with "they say," or "I know 'cause I saw it," or "I don't believe in 'em myself, but—" No matter how you feel about the validity of the paranormal, just about everyone enjoys a good ghost story.

The Hills of Judea in Augusta County are rich with such stories. At a place called Clamper Spring, in a "desolate, dreary hollow," there stood a gigantic ancient white oak tree, its branches spread wide. About fifty feet up the trunk there was a massive limb, worn smooth. It was said the devil sat on this branch at each full moon and dropped a chain for every sinner in the neighborhood that he would claim by death during the next lunar month. He appeared in the guise of a "great dragon," with saucer-like eyes that burned like the "headlights of an engine." No one ventured near this spring during the time of a full moon.[1]

Down along the Burkes Mill Road, near the edge of the Hills, there was a hardscrabble little place where a family named Sheets lived. Mrs. Sheets, who had been a Redner before she married, was thought to be peculiar. Every afternoon she tied chickens out in the woods around her house, "to keep the devil and wild spirits away." Apparently she thought they'd be satisfied with her offerings and would leave her alone.[2]

Cannon Woods

In the southern part of Clarke County, people avoided a certain stretch of woods after dark. Along the road that led down through Cannon Woods, named after a family that once owned them, toward a crossing of the Shenandoah River, many travelers reported seeing a ghost or ghosts in the form of eerie white mists.[3]

Jack-ma-lanterns

In neighboring Warren County, well-defined, sinister lights were reported in the forests after night had fallen. A native of these parts said, " 'Ol folks used to tell 'bout jack-ma-lanterns that 'ud lead you off at night. You know, back in those days there wasn't lights ever'where to guide a body like 'tis today. If you started to go somewhere at night you'd try to spot a light in some neighbor's house and foller that." Jack-ma-Lanterns were known to lead people into thickets or swamps. One way to avoid the lure of the faux lights was to turn your pockets inside out before starting on your journey.[4]

Chestnut Tree

In the 19th century, before a four lane highway whisked traffic through Page County, travelers on foot or horseback were confronted frequently by a spirit near the South Fork of the Shenandoah River as they approached the White House Bridge. A cabin stood near the spot in colonial times, and the story is that a woman and her children were killed there by Indians while her husband was away hunting. The only thing left to mark the site of the tragedy was a huge old chestnut tree, whose branches leaned out over the road.

When wayfarers neared the tree at dusk, their horses were likely to become skittish, and some travelers even refused to go on. The ones who continued their journey felt a definite presence as they passed the giant tree.

Sometimes, it is said, a woman comes out of the dusk or darkness and offers the traveler a pie. If a gesture of acceptance is made, she disappears with a peculiar sound, something like a sigh.[5]

Adam Kersh

The old road that crossed over from St. Michael's Church to the Wise Hollow road passed the cabinet shop of Adam Kersh. The shop was on the old family farm, which was run by Adam's married brother George, who was also a part-time blacksmith.

Adam was a life-long bachelor who lived above his shop. He was a congenial man, and the shop was a favorite gathering place for friends to pass an afternoon while he worked at the bench or lathe. He was fond of children, loved music and was renowned as a fiddle player. Adam made and repaired the instruments in his shop.

The furniture he made was a cut above what was usually produced in the backcountry. The lines and details in his case pieces and chairs showed that he had studied in youth under a master cabinetmaker. Besides furniture, he made farm implements, and for tools like grain cradles that also needed iron parts,

Adam Kersh (1828-1905),
the ghost of St. Michael's cemetery.

he collaborated with George. He created special pieces for children. One of his nieces remembered that when she was a little girl she went over to Uncle Ad's with her wagon, and he loaded a small desk onto it that he had made just for her.

When he went off to fight in the Civil War, in the 52nd Virginia Infantry, he took a fiddle with him. Whenever the opportunity allowed, he was encouraged by his fellow soldiers to play. In the terrible fighting between the armies of Lee and Grant in early 1864, he was wounded twice. The first time was in mid-May, during the battle of Spotsylvania Court House, near the infamous Bloody Angle; this was a slight wound to the head by a nearly spent bullet. On May 30th, at the battle of Bethesda Church, he was more seriously wounded, and more than half of his regiment was lost.[6]

He recovered from his wounds, and when the war ended, he returned to his trade of cabinetmaker. He was in great demand as a fiddle player at lawn parties and other social

Adam Kersh's gravestone

gatherings. He was often accompanied by "Fighting Bob" Misner; they were great friends and visited each other often.

Adam Kersh died on March 22, 1905, and was buried in St. Michael's Church Cemetery, but his story doesn't end there. On some clear nights, when there is a rustling sigh of wind through the tops of the trees, Adam Kersh sits on his tombstone and plays his fiddle. It has been heard over in Wise Hollow and into the Hills of Judea.[7]

Miller House

The Adam Miller house, near Elkton, in eastern Rockingham County, is reputed to be the oldest house in the Shenandoah Valley. Miller was the first settler of record. By the late 19th century, no one was living in the house, but it was used for storage by the family who lived in a farmhouse not far away. A girl named Yager came to visit the daughter of the family for a few days. One evening the girls were directed to go over to the old house to get some apples that were stored in the attic. They did what they were told, but they didn't like the idea very much because it was a lonely and spooky place, especially in the dark. This was before the time of electric lights, and the girls carried candles to light their way.

They gathered up a couple dozen apples in their aprons, and each girl held a candle in one hand and clutched her apron full of apples with the other as they started down the steep, creaky stairs. They were suddenly startled by a dark figure coming up the stairs, screamed in terror, and covered their eyes with the hands that had been securing the apples. The apples flew from the aprons and bounced down two flights of stairs, but met no obstruction.

The ghostly figure, they later discovered, was the first girl's shadow, cast by the candle of the girl descending behind her.[8]

Open Graves

It was the custom, in years gone by, to dig the grave for a burial the night before the funeral. On at least two occasions this led to heart-stopping experiences for children passing by the cemeteries at Ottobine and Bank churches in Rockingham County. As they passed the sites at dusk and looked out across the yard of tombstones, they were stunned to see something white rise from a freshly dug grave and then as quickly disappear. They were glued to the spot with fright until, in both cases, they realized that sheep had fallen into the hole and were trying vainly to get out.[9]

Brocks Gap

Up in the Brocks Gap region, the old residents referred to the rest of the world as "out." It was not uncommon to hear the phrase, "people would come along from out."[10]

In the old days, the rest of the county was well served by the Valley Pike and other well maintained thoroughfares, but the Gap and its scattered homesteads remained isolated beyond the first rise of the Allegheny Front. The hamlets of Fulks Run, Criders, Bergton and Dovesville were oases of social contact, as were a few churches here and there, but the people in the Gap were pretty self-sufficient. Before electricity came into the area, moonless nights smothered the hills, hollows and mountains with a thick curtain, making the faint glimmer of candlelight in a window way off a welcome sight to a late-night traveler.

It is not surprising that some wonderful ghost stories have come from this area. Unusual happenings were woven into stories that were told and retold throughout the community. Long winter nights found rapt listeners gathered around a glowing fire or warm stove to be thrilled by a storyteller.

One young girl of the Criders area was told that she could take the horse and go to meet her mother and sister, who were returning from a trip to "out" late one night. Her path took her to a neighbor's farm gate, where she dismounted, opened the gate, led the horse through and then re-latched it. As she climbed back on the horse, she heard something coming from the direction she had just come.

"Someone come a runnin', was a man a comin' up the road a runnin'."

He was coming fast and she was scared. She kicked her horse into a gallop. As she looked back over her shoulder she saw the "man" run through the closed gate as if he were made of air. "I flew out," she said, but it seemed to make no difference—he was gaining on her.

"When I got to the top of the hill he was about two steps behind me. He grabbed the horse by the tail, and she kicked up, and away she went as hard as she could run!"

That did the trick and the pursuer disappeared in their dust.

"I don't know what it was. It wasn't no human; no human coulda kept up with that horse!"

The woman who was once the girl in the preceding story also related her father's brush with a demon.

"My daddy seen one one time. He was comin' home after dark from Casper Turner's. Saw what looked like a man layin' on a fence; had eyes like fireballs!" Her father had a gun with him, and he shot at the demon. The thing fell off the fence and started making a noise that made the man think he should be getting away from there. "He run down from the mountain. He was scared to death."[11]

Henry Shickel

Henry Shickel, a veteran of the 7th Virginia Cavalry, had to go "out" for jury duty at the county seat in Harrisonburg on one occasion. The court wrapped up its business late in the afternoon, and Mr. Shickel decided to walk back to his home beyond the mountain. It was dark when he passed through Hopkins Gap and came down through the Mount Carmel Church section, but by that time a bright full moon had risen, and distinct shadows could be seen as he made his way along back country roads and cut across the fields. He was nearing home when he came into an area that the local inhabitants associated with ghosts and "people with no heads."

When passing through an orchard of old gnarled trees, he was startled and his blood froze as, "Behold, when I got halfway through those apple trees, something white came out of the shade and came walkin' right toward me." He thought to himself, "Well, I never done anything wrong, and I don't think I should run."

Henry put his faith in the notion that evil cannot touch a good man, and he was right—the apparition turned out to be a large white calf.[12]

Cry Baby Lane

Up near Fulks Run there is a haunted house back in the woods at the end of a dirt road called Cry Baby Lane. It is said that a baby was murdered there long ago by being buried alive. If you are brave enough, you can go back there late in the night, stand before the house, and sing out the way school children do: "Cry, baby, cry; cry, baby, cry!" Chances are you might hear the wail of a child from the dark depths of the house.

Many people have gone back there on various occasions over the years. Some have had flashlights go out; sometimes several at the same time.

Other people have become enveloped in chilled air, even in the summer. No one goes there alone.[13]

Eleven Thumps

There is a haunted house near Trissels Mennonite Church in western Rockingham County. A man was supposed to have been murdered there. People said that he was killed on the stair landing by decapitation; his head was supposed to have bounced down eleven steps.

The old house is, of course, deserted, and posted against trespassing, but many people ignore the signs and go in anyway to see if they can see or hear the ghost. One time, two people were standing in the hallway of the old house near the stairs when all of a sudden, out of the dead silence, they heard, "thump, thump, thump, thump, thump, thump, thump, thump, thump, thump and .... thump."[14]

Nothing

Down along Dry River, in the same county, there is a spot by the road where a black man was killed and buried so many years ago that no one remembers the circumstances of his death. People were afraid to pass the spot which was "in a corner of Shickel's field." Some would ask as they skittered by, "What did you do to be buried here?" He'd say ... nothing.[15]

Old Hedrick Place

Also in Rockingham, up near Rawley Springs, there used to be a two-story log house called the Old Hedrick Place. There was a tradition in the old days that a peddler was murdered there, at the top of the stairs. A patch of blood at that spot could not be scrubbed away. Another unsettling occurrence was that the covers could not be kept on the bed in the room the peddler was said to have used. Even with the door locked at night, in the morning the covers would be on the floor. No one would sleep in that room. Eventually all the furniture was removed, and the room was locked permanently.[16]

Old Grey Beard

Out on the old Northwestern Pike, west of Winchester in Frederick County, there was a two-story house where another peddler was rumored to have been murdered. Once, when a couple of children were in residence, he made himself known to them.

In one lower room there was an enclosed staircase with a door. The brother and sister often played in this particular room. They had heard the stories the adults told about the ghost, and they wanted to believe. One time, when they were playing with cut-out paper animals on a table in the room, the latch to the staircase door raised up and down, over and over again. The sound of the clicking metal aggravated the boy, and he called out, "Come on down, if your nose is clean!" Soon it was discovered that no one was on the staircase or in the room above.

The peddler's ghost appeared one night. The girl awakened in her room and saw a man with a long, grey beard leaning over her bed and staring at her intently. Hastily brushing the sleep from her eyes with the backs of her hands, she looked again, wide-eyed, and he was still there. She let out a gasp and threw the covers over her head, and when she got up nerve enough to look again, he had disappeared.

In the light of day, the little girl thought that the apparition must have been a dream, after all, but when she told her brother about it, he related that he, too, had been visited by the old, grey-bearded man.[17]

The Preachers' Ghost

In Bath County, near Zion Hill Church, a strange apparition of a man on a white horse has been observed many times through the years. The story was that it was the ghost of a traveler murdered on the road in the long ago. The ghost was seen for many years, and all of the reports were made by preachers.[18]

A preacher named Goodall was the first person to report a sighting. At dusk one evening he saw the form of a man on horseback as he was riding up a road near the church. He heard the sound of the horse before he actually saw the pair, but the vision was clear and not far ahead. Before the Reverend Goodall could get close enough to identify the rider, he rode out of sight around a bend in the road. The reverend hurried his own horse along, but when he got to the bend and looked down the long straight stretch of road ahead, he found it was empty. There was no sign of the mysterious rider and no evidence of a horse having just passed by. The preacher saw the ghost frequently, but he could never catch up to him.

Wizard Clip

One of the earliest and most well-documented cases of strange and diabolical manifestations occurred in the far northern Shenandoah Valley, in Jefferson County, West Virginia. The lovely village of Middleway, about seven miles from Charles Town, the seat of Jefferson County, was near the scene in 1794 of eerie happenings that seemed to be controlled by a restless, angry spirit. The settlement is also known as Wizard's Clip.

Adam Livingston came to the area in 1790 from Pennsylvania. He purchased a house and lot and acreage near the village, and it is said that he was quickly accepted in the community and prospered there. His happiness and contentment were soon destroyed, however.

Livingston took in a boarder, a stranger who, after residing in the house for some time, became seriously ill. The stranger, knowing he was near death, confided that he was a Catholic and needed to see a priest before he died. Livingston was horrified; "papists" were not held in high regard in the staunchly Protestant Valley. The landlord informed his boarder in no uncertain terms that there probably wasn't a Catholic priest south of the Potomac, and even if there were, he wouldn't allow one to enter his house.

The poor papist was failing quickly, and again he asked Mr. Livingston to summon a priest for the sake of his soul. Livingston was unmoved, and the request was denied for the second and last time.

The man died, but apparently did not cross over to the other side. A village man was hired to keep vigil with the corpse that night. The candle he carried into the closed room was snuffed out almost immediately, and although he tried to light several other tapers, these, too, refused to stay lighted. He fled the room and reported the weird occurrence to his employer. That incident was tame when compared with what was to follow.

The next night galloping horses were heard racing around the dwelling, but nothing could be seen. The boarder was buried with haste, but still would not rest.

Within a week, the Livingstons' barn had burned to cinders, and all of their cattle died. In the house, pottery and furniture fell and moved on their own. Glowing embers flew from fireplaces and bounced around the rooms. Money thought to have been put away in a secure place came up missing. It was said that the heads of all the poultry on the place "fell off."

Next the spirit took up invisible scissors, and sounds of snipping and clipping could be heard. Blankets, sheets, boots, clothing and saddles were all clipped—all snipped with crescent-shaped slits. The unsettling activities continued for several months, and word spread across the county about Mr. Livingston's unwelcome guest.

An old woman from Martinsburg came over to satisfy her curiosity about the ghostly doings. She knew of the spirit's disposition to cut things up, so she folded her fine silk cap into a pocket to protect it. But to no avail—by the time she left, it was in shreds.

Livingston called in several witch doctors, who were powerless against the determined presence. He was greatly agitated and forlorn—and then he had a dream. In it he climbed a steep mountain with great difficulty, but he persevered and gained the summit. There he saw a man in flowing robes, and a voice whispered in his ear, "This is the man who can relieve you." When he awoke, his thoughts immediately turned to an Episcopal clergyman he had heard about in Winchester. Episcopalians, he knew, wore robes during services. He journeyed to see that worthy gentleman, but he was nothing like the man in his dream.

At this point in his desperation, Livingston thought back to the boarder's original request, sought out a Catholic family he knew about, and asked after a priest. They told him that a priest was to be in Shepherdstown the following Sunday. There Livingston met Father Dennis Cahill. He told his story to the priest, and the two returned together to Wizard's Clip. Father Cahill uncorked his bottle of holy water and sprinkled the home and property, but the spirit demanded more. He would not rest until the priest conducted a full mass, after which he vacated the premises forever. Adam Livingston now had his peace but he had lost his desire for the place, sold out and returned to Pennsylvania.[19]

The site is currently owned by the Catholic church and is operated as a retreat.

McChesney's Ghost

Another well-documented incident occurred in 1825, when Dr. John McChesney, his wife, family and their servants lived in pastoral tranquility near the village of Newport in southwestern Augusta County. Dr.

McChesney was esteemed and respected in the Upper Valley, and his reputation for honesty was beyond question.

While still deep in the winter months, the McChesney's were having supper one night, when a young slave girl named Maria burst into the house from the direction of the detached kitchen. She was frightened and said that an old woman had chased her in a threatening manner. The woman was described as having "her head tied up," which must have meant that she had her head bound with a scarf or cloth. The description did not fit anyone on the place, and the family passed off the incident as fancy.

In the next few days, however, Maria was seen to be fearful and easily startled. Dr. McChesney and the rest of the family began to take an intense interest in matters concerning the girl when stones started to fall on the roof from out of nowhere. This happened both day and night, and at times the stones were observed to be hot, as they scorched the dry grass when they fell from above.

The story of the strange happenings at the McChesneys' became common knowledge in the surrounding countryside. It was said that hundreds of people would surround the house in the hope of witnessing a stone fall. It is not clear if they saw anything, for on some days nothing out of the ordinary occurred. Maria continued to be frightened and said that she was being chased by the old woman who remained unseen by others.

Dr. McChesney thought that the girl might be tied to everything that was happening, so one day he sent her over to the home of his brother-in-law, Thomas Steele.

Mrs. Steele, her children, a young white woman and a black washer woman were out in the yard doing chores that day, and Mr. Steele was away from home. Suddenly loud noises were heard from the house. It sounded like frightened horses were loose in the structure. The young woman ran to the door and called for Mrs. Steele to come look—all of the furniture was piled in a jumble in the center of the room. As if they weren't startled enough already, stones then began to fall on the roof of the dwelling.

At that moment Maria was spotted coming toward them from over the hills. They ran to meet her and found the girl in terror as she related her story of being pursued, although no one was to be seen behind her. Mrs. Steele immediately sent Maria back to the McChesneys.

Even after the girl was sent away, stones continued to fall at the Steele home. Some even entered the house and broke the glass in the doors of a cupboard. Many plates and other dishes were broken, and some of the shards were saved for many years as relics of the terrible incidents.

Back at the McChesneys, strange things continued to occur as the weeks passed into early spring. One of the most singular episodes took place on a cool day as Dr. and Mrs. McChesney, Mrs. Mary Steele, Mr. and Mrs. Thomas Steele and their young son, William, were sitting around a fireplace. All of the doors and windows were securely shut, when suddenly a stone seemed to fly from an upper corner of the room, hitting Mrs. Thomas Steele on the head. She was the only person struck. The wound was deep and bled profusely, and a lock of hair was cut cleanly off, as if someone had used scissors. Her husband was enraged and took the invisible assailant to task by shouting that its spite should have been directed at him instead of a defenseless woman. He then sat in a chair near the door and was almost immediately showered with missiles of sod and earth from within the room. His mother, Mary Steele, shouted that he would be killed and urged him to leave the room. He did so and was not followed by the "thing."

It was decided to send the children of both families out of harm's way, and they went with their grandmother to her home near the hamlet of Midway. Their error was in also sending Maria along.

Soon Mary Steele's home was in turmoil with stones flying about and the furniture in the kitchen being moved by unseen hands. One day a bench in the kitchen bucked about like a playful colt. Only the children were present, and they were at first amused. Young John Steele decided to ride the bench, but the effort was more than he had bargained for. He fainted and was taken from the room by the rest of the children, who had become scared of the out-of-control object.

During the time the children were with their grandmother, her farm hands complained that tools and food they had taken with them to the fields were stolen—but the missing goods turned up later, back at the house.

The little slave girl complained to Mrs. Steele that she was being beaten. The kind old lady drew the child toward her and wrapped her skirts around her while she struck out at the air with her cane. Maria still cried that she was being hit and stabbed with pins. Young William Steele remembered when he was an old man that the slaps could be distinctly heard by all who were present. The child was tormented for many weeks.

Dr. McChesney, at his wit's end, finally sold Maria south. When the child left, everything returned to normal, and Maria was undisturbed in her new home.

William Steele related in later years that an old black woman who lived in their neighborhood was rumored to be a witch. He described her by saying that, "She walked with a stick and chewed tobacco," and that whenever he met her in the road, he always yielded to her the right of way. William said that Maria had once spoken to the old woman in an insulting manner and was told in reply that she would be punished for her disrespectful tongue.[20]

Dancing Fire Tongs

Another story about the McChesney place concerns a man who had a run-in with a pair of dancing fire tongs. The man had been sitting peacefully by his hearth when all of a sudden the tongs left their place and started to dance about, mystifying the observer. He got to his feet, grabbed the tongs and put them back in their normal spot as he yelled, "Get back there, damn you!" They immediately jumped out again and danced around the room. The man grabbed them a second time, but there was a struggle and magically the tongs burned the man on his left leg.

No one knows how the wounded man finally resolved the problem of the unruly tongs. The scar on the man's leg looked fresh for years, just as if he were newly burned.[21]

A Distinctive Step

In the upper Shenandoah Valley there is a house near a battlefield. The old dwelling, which has been in the same family for more than a hundred years, has seen many happy times, but it has also been under the storm clouds of war. It is haunted by the shade of one of the combatants of the Civil War, whose spirit has become a part of the family.

This ghost doesn't go out of his way to frighten—he just likes to roam, and his distinctive footfall has been heard crossing the hardwood floors in daylight as well as after dark. He wears a sword, and the thump of the scabbard can be heard after every step. Residents of the house accept the ghost's presence and are comfortable with him.

An older woman, who had lived the greater part of her life in the house, thought of the ghost as an old friend. On one occasion, she invited one of her friends to stay over for a few days. After spending a congenial first evening together visiting and catching up on old times, they retired to separate rooms for the night, the guest in an upstairs room and her hostess downstairs because she couldn't take stairs very well anymore.

A little later the woman, who knew every sigh and creak of the floorboards, heard the ghost walking. She wondered if her friend heard him, and she worried that she might be frightened as she had told her about the family's ghost. She listened intently and after a few minutes decided her friend was sound asleep, so she closed her eyes, too.

The next morning at breakfast the woman asked her guest if she had slept well.

"Yes, I slept like a top," her friend answered.

"Did you hear anything?"

"No, went right to sleep," the friend said.

They spent another nice day together and were both tired when it came time for bed. The lady of the house fell to sleep almost immediately, and nothing disturbed her slumber.

The next morning at breakfast she again asked her friend how she had passed the night.

"Well," she said, "I fell asleep pretty quickly, but was awakened by the footsteps. At first I was a bit scared, and then I realized it was you moving around downstairs. What were you doing up and about so late, anyway?"

"Why do you think it was me?"

"I knew it was you when I heard the thump of your cane," the friend replied.

"I slept the night through," the woman told her. "You heard our ghost and the thump of his sword."[22]

Where There's Smoke ...

There is a house in Bridgewater that was built by one of the town's entrepreneurs, D. S. Thomas, in 1899. He also built a washhouse and a small combination stable and barn to the rear of the property. The house was home to Thomas and his wife and two children, and his mother-in-law also lived there. It's his mother-in-law that this little tale is about. She was a tiny, old country woman who wore long black dresses and a poke bonnet. She also smoked a pipe, which she had done nigh all her life.

Now, Mr. Thomas was rightly proud of his new house and didn't want it burned to the ground by an old lady falling asleep while smoking a pipe. He forbade her to smoke in the dwelling, so she went outside to smoke, and, if the weather was bad, she'd go to the barn and fire up her bowl of tobacco. She did this for years and was content with the arrangement 'til the day she died.

The barn stood until 1974, and people affirmed that at times, especially on days of rain or snow, you could smell fresh pipe smoke in the old building.[23]

Dark Being

Between Dayton and Bridgewater, sometime around Christmas in 1901, there were reports of a dark being standing by the road in the dead of night. Apparently it threatened no one, but it was not considered human, and for a few weeks there was a general uneasiness in that part of Rockingham County.

In Harrisonburg one night, a stranger stopped by C. L. Jordan's livery stable on German Street and requested to be driven out to Bridgewater. Mr. Jordan harnessed a team and carriage and asked Follinsbe Welcher to accompany them, so he'd have a companion on the return trip.

The three men drove along quietly for some time. They passed Dayton and were on the upgrade toward Herrings Hill when they beheld the dark form that had terrified the countryside by its mere silent presence. It stood close by the road, featureless. Mr. Jordan was a brave soul, and he sprang from the carriage to investigate. He grabbed the creature, but was overpowered by an unnatural strength and could do no more than call for help. Mr. Welcher rushed to his aid, only to find his added strength to be insufficient in contending with this entity. The unequal contest lasted for several minutes, and the two liverymen were left sprawled on the ground. The creature, the dark, unyielding form, had melted away into the night.

Mr. Jordan and Mr. Welcher pulled themselves together, and, finding that they had no major injuries, they re-entered the carriage and drove the mystified stranger on to Bridgewater. On the return trip to Harrisonburg, Mr. Jordan whipped up the team to a "three minute pace" as they passed the place of the encounter with the unearthly fiend.[24]

Hospitality

At Lebanon Springs, on the old wagon trail leading up to Jennings Gap in the Allegheny Front, there is a house that has seen much history. It was the home of an innkeeper in the early days of the West Augusta community, and it has passed through the hands of several local families over the years.

A tradition of hospitality seems to come with the house, as it has entertained travelers in its own right for as long as anyone can remember. In the decades following the Civil War, it was known as Ye Old Coffee House. Many drovers and travelers stopped to refresh themselves as they passed between Virginia and West Virginia.[25] It was a place everyone remembered fondly.

One person, either a former visitor or, more likely, an earlier resident, decided to stay on forever. Frances Griffin, the present owner, has heard distinct footsteps on the staircase on many different occasions when no one else was present. These ghostly sounds happen in the day as well as at night. Mrs. Griffin and her family have never felt threatened, and Mr. Griffin once actually saw the apparition of a young woman, but only briefly.

One morning Mrs. Griffin entertained a teacher friend. They were having coffee and sharing stories when they heard someone climbing the stairs. The visitor, who thought that they were alone, asked his hostess who else was in the house. Mrs. Griffin answered matter-of-factly, "That's my little ghost, Margaret." The skeptical young man left the table and hurried up the stairs, where he searched everywhere without finding anyone else.

The only time the ghost deviated from her stair climbing routine was when the teacher was visiting again, this time with his wife and young daughter. As they sat chatting with Mrs. Griffin, a piece of hard candy flew through the air, apparently from nowhere, and hit the wall beside the little girl's head. It can only be hoped that the incident was a poor attempt on the ghost's part to befriend the child.[26]

Hungry Ghost

Hickory Dale, one of the earliest farms to be settled in the Deerfield Valley of western Augusta County, is the ancestral home of the Clayton family. John Clayton, the pioneer, is said to have been the son of an English lord.

Following the War Between the States, the Claytons then living on the place told their former slaves that they were welcomed to stay on as hired hands or, if they so chose, they could leave and try to start new lives elsewhere. Among the freedmen were the Claytons' old mammy and her grown son, Jake. The two had been favorites with the Clayton children because they told wonderful ghost stories around the kitchen fireplace.

Eventually Jake took his mother and moved away. They traveled far from the bountiful Deerfield Valley and saw hard times as Jake tried to establish a new life for them. His mother often went hungry and sorely missed the food that had always been in abundance at Hickory Dale.

She sent word through someone to her former master that she would like to return home. The Claytons would have sent for her, but before they could do so, they received a message that the old woman had died.

Perhaps she actually began the journey back to her old home in Virginia at the moment of her death, because soon a strange, continuous haunting began at Hickory Dale, involving an old cupboard in the kitchen that had always been well stocked with food. On uncounted mornings, the door to the cupboard, which was usually latched, was found standing open. The blacks who had remained on the farm began to whisper that Mammy had returned and was getting something to eat.

The old woman's hunger must have been remarkable, because she raided the larder for close to fifty years before her craving was finally appeased. The cupboard is still in the Clayton family, but now the door remains closed.[27]

Pulsing Spring

Bellevue, an estate near Shepherdstown in the lower Valley, was the home of Revolutionary War veteran Colonel Joseph Van Swearingen. There is a legend that Catawba Indians captured an enemy Delaware chief near a spring on the property and fiendishly buried him alive. The waters from the spring spurt instead of flow; people say that it does so because of the beating heart of the buried chief.[28]

Open the Latch

A log house in the town of Edinburg in Shenandoah County has a poltergeist, a spirit that creates noisy disturbances and moves things without being seen. This particular log house was built beside Stoney Creek in the 1700s and was later moved to higher ground and renovated. A couple from Virginia Beach, Phill and Pam Ungar, purchased it and rented it to friends. They visited the Valley occasionally and spent a few days in the old place as guests.

One evening, after supper, both couples sat around the kitchen table playing cards. In one end of the room there is an enclosed staircase, typical in a house of this age, that leads up to a room where the logs are still exposed. The small door opening to the stairs has its original hardware, including an outside metal drop latch.

Suddenly the door to the staircase flew open and startled them. Phill remarked that a window must be open in the room above and that a good breeze must be up. "Oh, that's just the ghost," said one of the tennants.

Phill said that he thought ghosts walked through closed doors, but he was informed that this one lifted the latch and opened the door and did it quite frequently. Phill checked the hardware, then closed the door and saw that it was securely shut when the latch was down.

Curious, Pam and Phill moved their chairs over to a spot directly in front of the door, where they could observe the latch close up. In about five minutes they saw the bar move up and the door swing open. The staircase was empty.[29]

Brothers

When you come down out of Hopkins Gap traveling westward, you pass Gospel Hill Church. Many people in that area at one time did not believe in airing their business in court, so differences frequently were settled face-to-face, in a violent manner. Such was the case with two Roadcap brothers who lived near the church property long ago. Apparently there was a dispute between them as to which one had inherited a certain mill.

The story is told that the brothers met in a barn not far from the church one night and joined in a fight to the death. The combat was vicious, but nothing was settled, as both brothers died from their wounds. The minister at Gospel Hill Church refused the brothers burial in the cemetery because he was disgusted with the manner of their deaths, so they were interred just outside of the churchyard fence, in unmarked graves. Even today, people passing by the church in the night sometimes hear the sounds of the terrible fight, as do people living near the old barn.[30]

Jess Craig

Jess Craig was a moonshiner who lived on a mountain in western Rockingham County. He was known to be fond of his own product. When he died, his house passed through several hands and was finally abandoned.

The series of folks who tried to make their home there eventually lost their nerve and moved away. They said that every morning they'd hear the ghost of old Jess coughing and clearing his throat as he awakened. But what *really* put them off was when the coughing and clearing was followed by Jess's voice asking for a drink of whiskey.[31]

Mapleton

To close this chapter we offer the continuing story of Mapleton, a house that was built on a hill known as "The Coaling," a foothill of the Blue Ridge Mountains in eastern Rockingham County, so called because it was the site of a charcoal making operation in the early to mid-19th century. The hill, once part of a huge tract of land granted to Thomas Lewis in 1751,[32] was a place of strategic importance during the Civil War battle of Port Republic in 1862. This, however, is not a story of war; it is about families.

In 1886 a Lewis descendant built the house, which was used for many years as a summer residence by five Lewis sisters, two of whom spent their winters in Baltimore and Memphis respectively, but all of whom eventually moved into the house permanently. They must have been very attached to the old place. Some people think that they may never have left.

It is a lovely spot, surrounded by trees and forest ravines where ferns and wildflowers grow. In the winter and early spring there is a wonderful view across a broad field that leads down to the South Fork of the Shenandoah River. The sisters and many others enjoyed sitting on the porch in the quiet of a spring evening.

In an early springtime years later, in 1979, as a matter of fact, a young couple who had purchased Mapleton spent their first day arranging furniture and unpacking boxes of household items. They worked well into the evening, until weariness overtook them, and they settled down to sleep. They had hardly begun to doze when they were awakened by the gentle sound of women talking among themselves. The Coaling is remote, with no near neighbors, and try as they might, they never could account for the voices.

On another occasion, the husband was awakened by a knocking. He had opened the bedroom door and stepped into the hall on his way

Two of the Lewis sisters of Mapleton playing croquet on the lawn.

downstairs to answer the front door when his mind cleared of sleep and he realized that the knocking had been at their own bedroom door.

The knocking was repeated the next night. On the third night, as they made ready to retire, the wife suggested that they leave the door open and see what might happen. The knocking ceased and never resumed.[33]

One of the most fascinating incidences in the house was the mysterious disappearance of a ring. The wife removed her ring only when she was working in the kitchen or when she cleaned the bathroom. In the kitchen, she placed it on top of the refrigerator, and in the bathroom, she put it on a shelf of the linen closet. But on this day, the ring was not in either place.

The woman searched the kitchen from top to bottom, even moved the refrigerator, but found no sign of the ring. She searched the linen closet, and then inspected every piece of linen in it, piece by piece. Again, her efforts were in vain. She delayed in telling her husband that the ring was gone, hoping it would materialize, but after two weeks she gave up and told her husband about the loss.

That evening she needed something from the linen closet. Almost immediately her eye fell on her errant ring sitting on the top of a pile of folded towels—towels that had been used and washed since the first search.

Her husband is known to many as a most honorable man, and he asserts that he had nothing to do with the disappearance or the miraculous reappearance of his wife's ring.[34]

In 1993, Mapleton was sold again, and the new owners and their daughter took possession that fall. On the first day they moved hardly anything in. The house was essentially empty, except for a mattress on the floor in the master bedroom and a sleeping bag in the daughter's room.

At 3:00 a.m. the wife awakened to the low growling of a small dog they had in the bedroom with them. She could hear, in what seemed like the far distance, a woman's laughter. Her husband seemed not to have been disturbed, so she quieted the dog and went back to sleep. In the morning she asked him if he had heard anything unusual in the night. He replied that he had heard a woman laughing at some point but hadn't thought much about it.

About a month later, early in the morning, the woman was descending the stairs to start breakfast; her two cats were just in front of her. They were all about halfway down when a door slammed below. The cats froze in their tracks, as did the woman momentarily. She rushed back upstairs, closely followed by the cats, to get her husband. She was afraid that there was a burglar in the house.

When the couple inspected the first floor they found everything in place and all of the outside doors securely locked.[35]

It seems as if the Lewis sisters are letting subsequent owners of the house know of their presence, though they appear to be willing to share the premises.

Gypsies

Several bands of gypsies appeared in the Shenandoah Valley in the 19th century, roving from Bath County in the south to Warren County in the north. These were the true Romany gypsies of Europe, descendants of tribes long settled in the British Isles. Specific information pertaining to these bands, such as dates and names, is difficult to ascertain; it's part of their culture to be evasive when questioned by outsiders. One informant in Rockingham County observed that "they'd tell the truth sometimes, when it didn't suit them to tell somethin' else."[1]

The gypsies of Rockingham were in the county by about 1850, with the last few members of the group moving away in the early 1930s. The various bands of Valley gypsies were inter-related; there is some evidence of marriages and of visiting back and forth among the families.

The Rockingham gypsies were from one of the three main tribes of English gypsies, the Stanleys. Their primary camp was near the hamlet of Lilly in the southwest quadrant of the county. It was described as a village of tents with stovepipes sticking out of them, both summer and winter. Some gypsies referred to houses as "tents of stone."

There were about sixty members of this particular band—men, women and children—and they were described as being rather drab in appearance.[2] In the spring they moved down Dry River, to the vicinity of the village of Rushville, for the pussy willows that bloomed along Muddy Creek. The young shoots were most pliant in the springtime, and the gypsies wove them into baskets to sell for cash or trade for food and other necessities from farms and stores. Some of the baskets were wholly woven from the willow, and some had solid wood bottoms that were cut out for them by a local Mennonite woodworker.[3] During the summer and early fall they moved around mending pots and pans at farms—they had a particular knack for it.

What the gypsies most enjoyed doing, though, was trading horses. There were regular horse fairs held in various towns at that time. A noted one was held annually at Timberville, in north-central Rockingham. The streets were crowded from side to side and end to end with horses, farmers, livestock dealers, blacksmiths and farriers—and the gypsies, who were famous for their ability to come out ahead in a trade. Everyone complained about how sharp they were, but tried to beat them at their own game anyway. One country woman said she thought that "they could trade you out of your shoes." She also admitted that "my daddy got whipped pretty good in a horse deal with 'em."[4]

Even with their daily presence in the community, the gypsies were looked upon as alien beings, and they were mostly ignored unless they were in a position where they could not otherwise be avoided. Fraternization between gypsies and Valley folk was extremely uncommon except when doing business. One noted exception was the romance between a stockman named Burk McCall from the Sangerville area of Augusta County and a gypsy princess.[5]

In the last quarter of the 19th century, McCall journeyed to Elkins, West Virginia, for the annual week-long, horse fair sponsored by that town. Soon after his arrival, McCall saw a pretty gypsy girl, a princess among her people, and lost his heart. The beautiful Ms. Harrison (her given name has been lost in time), took a strong attraction to him, too, and by the end of the week he had proposed marriage. She told him that her band would never permit such a union and worried that if they got wind of his intentions, they might do him harm.

He assured her that he had a plan for their safe passage, and they made ready to flee to his home in the Shenandoah Valley. Soon the lovers were off, flying at top speed over the winding mountain roads on two of McCall's best horses. McCall knew that the gypsy men, riding their fine horses, would set off in pursuit as soon as they became aware of the elopement, and indeed, it wasn't long before the gypsies were hot on the trail.

McCall's plan relied on his knowledge of horses and his reputation as a superb judge of horseflesh to counter the hostile intentions of those who followed. He'd push his horses to a point just before they began to show signs of breaking down, then he'd stop and trade the sleek mounts to some farmer or stockman for fresh horses. This he did several times, and they arrived at his home well before the angry pursuers.

When the gypsies finally showed up, they found that McCall and his princess had already been wed. The union changed McCall's status with the band, even though they had initially opposed it. It had, in point of fact, made him one of them. The group eventually settled in north-western Augusta County, and McCall, who had several stock farms in Augusta and Rockingham, became their protector. He was known ever after as "Gypsy" McCall.[6]

Dilly Stanley, the leader of the gypsy band centered on Lilly, has always been known as the Gypsy Queen of Ottobine. Finding the truths in her life is difficult. Her obituary states that she was born in 1848, but her grave marker indicates that she was born in 1835. She was married several times, to men named Broadaway, Kelly and Cooper (the name on her marker), but the name Dilly Stanley is the one she was best known by.[7]

Dilly became a part of Shenandoah Valley folklore at the end of the Civil War. About a week after Lee surrendered to Grant at Appomattox, the Gypsy Queen showed up at the home of Elizabeth Heatwole, about a mile up the road from Bank Church on Dry River. When Elizabeth answered the knock at her door, the gypsy said, "Mrs. Heatwole, you've got a red coverlet I've always admired, and if you'll give it to me, I'll tell your fortune."

Elizabeth answered that she didn't believe in fortune telling. The Queen of the Gypsies thought about it for a moment and then said, "Well, I'll tell your fortune anyway, and if you think it's worthwhile, you can give me the coverlet." She told the skeptical Elizabeth, "You've got two men off because of the war. Tonight they'll both come home. One'll come a walkin', and one'll come a ridin'. One'll have money in his pockets, and one'll have none."

Her prediction given, she left, heading along the river toward Lilly.

Just after dark Elizabeth's husband, "Potter John" Heatwole, came walking in from the western mountains. He had been working in the orchards of West Virginia. Some people said he had gone as far west as Ohio. The important point for this story is that he had his wages in his pockets.

Later that night Elizabeth's brother-in-law, Frank Murray, a Confederate cavalryman, came riding in from east Virginia on a bony old horse. His unit had disbanded after the surrender, and he'd made his way back to Rockingham County slowly, while searching for free food for man and beast in a countryside picked nearly clean by passing armies. Of course, he had not a penny to his name.

Here the story ends, unfortunately, for no one can remember whether or not Dilly Stanley was given the red coverlet.[8]

Copper grave marker of Dilly Stanley Cooper, the Gypsy Queen.

In 1910, Dilly became critically ill, and word of her condition spread through the surrounding farms and villages.

Two local girls, Fannie Jane Richard and Stella Newman, were curious about the well-known gypsy. It was May, so they gathered lilacs and then walked to the camp at Lilly to pay their respects to the dying queen. They were allowed to see her for a few minutes and to present their tribute of flowers. They remembered their visit and related it to family and friends for the rest of their lives.

Soon after the girls left, her followers for some reason decided to take the queen to the camp of the gypsies at Sangerville, about ten miles away. They carried her only as far as the Beaver Creek bridge, near Judge Paul's house, in the shadow of the ridge where the Ottobine Church stands. Before they crossed the creek, Dilly Stanley passed away.[9]

Arrangements were made to bury the queen in the Ottobine Cemetery. Two local ministers officiated at the service, which was followed by the destruction of her property by the members of her band.

The Harrisonburg *Daily Times* of Friday, May 17, 1910, describes in some detail the destruction of Dilly Stanley's personal belongings. "Valuable jewelry, dishes, clothing, including the finest handmade laces and valuable silks, and beautiful tapestry were burned. Even the wagon in which she made her home, a gaudy and gorgeous affair costing over six hundred dollars, was fed to the flames." In addition to noting the costliness of the effects sacrificed in the ritual, the newspaper informed its readers that the queen's two pet parrots were spared.

Her famous white horse, however, was chloroformed. In some circles it was said that the horse was buried with the queen, but it is highly unlikely that the ministers would have permitted such an act in consecrated ground.[10]

Since her interment, about a half-dozen other gypsies have been laid to rest near their queen.

Burk McCall died in 1915, while on a trip to Mecklenburg County. It was remembered that his coffin arrived at the depot in Bridgewater with a fifty dollar bill pinned to his suit and a note that read, "bury him beside the Gypsy Queen." It is probable that the reference to the "Gypsy Queen," meant the Harrison princess he had married, who had most likely become queen of the local gypsies at Dilly Stanley's death. He was buried in the Sangerville Cemetery.[11]

The stories of Dilly Stanley and Burk McCall have become tangled and confused in the ensuing years. It is certain that Dilly's story started years earlier than Burk's, though they surely knew each other.

The War

To this day, when Valley natives mention "the War," they don't mean anything but the Civil War; it is just understood. The war and all of its inherent horrors was the defining moment in the history of the Shenandoah Valley as it was for the rest of the nation. Feelings still run high, and if Union general Philip Sheridan's name is spoken, stony looks are forthcoming.

Until recently, there were still a few people living in almost every community who had heard from their own parents and grandparents first-hand accounts of how they were affected by that momentous era of discord. Their personal stories were handed down orally, and with the passage of time most will fade away unless they are recorded.

In the South, even the most well-documented history of individuals or events at times takes on the hazy aura of legend or folklore; "lost causes" lend themselves readily to romance. During dramatic periods, incidents occur that are beyond the bounds of the normal experiences of most people. Some are simply inexplicable—even when viewed in the context of war. These stories cannot be proved or disproved by established research techniques, therefore they are categorized as folklore. This is not to say that they should be dismissed, however, because it is likely that at the root of each is a kernel of truth.

Civil War stories about the Shenandoah Valley are interesting because they came into being on the periphery of or outside of the main theater of conflict and yet were wholly influenced by the war's unwavering grip on the collective psyche of the nation. Perhaps more so than in any other area, they have been preserved in minute detail because descendants of the original tellers are still on the land.

The war did not come to the Valley with ease. In principle, most of the Valley counties sent elected representatives to vote against the secession ordinance in Richmond in the spring of 1861.

When Abraham Lincoln called on the states to send troops to put down the insurrection in South Carolina, sentiment in the Shenandoah changed almost overnight. Virginia would not be a party to the coercion of another state and would not allow federal troops to traverse the commonwealth to impose the Lincoln administration's will on southern belligerents. Virginia withdrew from the Union on April 17, 1861.

In the Valley, many people were saddened that the United States would be torn asunder, yet they could not support the government in power. The population in general soon was gripped with patriotic spirit. There were, however, pockets of Mennonites, Dunkards, Quakers and anti-slavery mountain people who were less than enthusiastic about the position they were expected to support. They were looked upon by their neighbors with suspicion as being "Union men." Most of these people kept their own council; it became dangerous to express an opinion contrary to the prevailing one.

Early on, at a store in eastern Rockingham County, a patron entered who did not show the degree of enthusiasm for the coming war that his neighbors thought proper; he strongly opposed the secession movement. Someone asked him in a snide manner if he planned to go to war. The man answered quickly that he was "going to wait 'til the fire-eaters go." The storekeeper grabbed a two-pound weight from the counter top and was about to hurl it at the blasphemer's head but was restrained by a friend while others whisked the target out of the building.[1]

In many circles feelings ran extremely high, while in others people waited for the storm to come, unable to imagine the changes it would bring to their lives. With the significant movement of troops during Jackson's spring campaign of 1862, incidents occurred in the Valley that were remembered long after hostilities ceased.

Minnie Hedrick

Little Minnie Hedrick, five and a half years old, a bright, out-going child, lived on a road that ran past her house toward the hamlet of Cross Keys in Rockingham County. A swing hung from a sturdy branch of the pear tree in one corner of her yard.

It had rained for days on end in early June of 1862, but the weather had finally cleared enough for Min to swing in the spring air. When horsemen came sloughing down the mired track heading east, she jumped off her swing and ran to the fence.

A few of the horsemen stopped in the road, and Min opened the gate and went out among the animals. She got the attention of an officer and pointed toward Cross Keys. "You had better not go down the road there," she warned him. "It's very muddy." The man smiled. "Little girl, I've been in mud worse than that," he said gently, and then added, "You're too pretty to be out here among all these horses. You'd better go back to your yard."

Minnie Hedrick

With Min safely out of the road, the officer and his men rode on. Min, fascinated by the exchange, asked one of the last mounted men to pass who the man was that she had spoken to. "Stonewall Jackson," he replied.

All through her long life Minnie Hedrick cherished the experience and told her story of speaking with Stonewall Jackson in the road in front of her house. It was recounted in her obituary in 1956; she was ninety-nine years old when she died.[2]

George Sipe

Nine-year-old George Sipe kept out of sight, along with everyone else in the neighborhood, as the forces of Jackson and Shields hammered away at each other in the fields and on the foothills between the village of Port Republic and the Blue Ridge Mountains. Once the guns fell silent and an unearthly quiet reigned for a time, the inhabitants of the area emerged from their places of safety.

The aftermath of the fighting stunned them. After the months of talk, here was war on their own doorsteps—and it was grim in the extreme.

Abandoned equipment and weapons and the decaying bodies of horses and men were strewn everywhere.

George, his father, and David Gilmore, a neighbor, walked over the main battlefield, near the Lewis house. As they walked along, Mr. Gilmore told them that earlier that morning his wife had found a federal soldier in their yard helping himself to some honey from one of their hives. When he saw Mrs. Gilmore coming toward him, he said, "Old woman don't you want some honey? You look damned hungry." After he had his fill, he broke off a sprig of blooming phlox and stuck it with a flourish into his cap. He then went on his way, toward the scene of battle.

Near Lewis Run, George and the men saw the body of a northern soldier whose leg had been taken off at the thigh by a cannonball. The sight sickened them, but suddenly the brutality of war really hit home when David Gilmore pointed to something by the side of the road—a Yankee cap with a faded sprig of phlox in the band.[3]

Scared to Death

A story has come down about a reluctant soldier who, on the night before the battle of Port Republic, was heard raving near his camp. He had been recently conscripted into the Confederate service and was not able to square his situation in his own mind. Another soldier came along and asked what was wrong. The fainthearted man answered that he "was scared to death." He lamented that he never wanted to go to war, that he couldn't fight and would "be shot down like a dog." The terrified man beseeched the Almighty to have mercy on his soul.

The other soldier tried to encourage the man and get him to stand to his duty. His effort to reason with the man had no effect, and he lost his patience, calling the shaken man a coward and telling him he should be ashamed of himself. He finished up by declaring that the man was behaving "worse than a big baby!"

With this the unwilling recruit cried out, "Baby, you say; I wish I *was* a baby—and a gal baby, too!"[4]

Potter John Heatwole

Another reluctant rebel was Potter John Heatwole of western Rockingham County. He was called "Potter" John, a reference to his skill and trade, to distinguish him from several other John Heatwoles in the area.

He was a practical man and saw from the beginning that the South was in for a long struggle,[5] so early on he enlisted for a year in a regiment that would become a part of the Stonewall Brigade. His understanding was that after serving his time he could return home and live in peace.

When he left, he told his wife Elizabeth not to worry, that the time would pass quickly, and he would not take another man's life. He later told of standing in the ranks in line of battle and firing his rifle high to avoid hitting anyone.

Potter John Heatwole (1826-1907)
A wartime photo

At the end of his enlistment year the Confederacy enacted a conscription law, and Potter John was drafted for three additional years, even though at thirty-six he was a year above the age limit set by the act. This, he felt, was unfair. He tried to get out of the army through regular channels, but his petitions and pleas were ignored.

Four months later, following the battle of Cedar Mountain, he "detached" himself from Jackson's Corps and walked to his home beyond the Blue Ridge.[6] For a while he hid in a haystack near his house and pottery shop and visited his family by night.

The Confederate authorities worried that Potter John would become an example to young Mennonite and Dunkard men and encourage them to avoid military service. An organized drive to capture him was formed,[7] and a price was put on his head. For the next two years Potter John, who was a noted hunter before the war, played a cat and mouse game with the squads sent out by the county provost marshal to find him.[8]

He left home again and went into the mountains that he knew like the back of his hand. He erected several huts in various ravines in the first rises of the Allegheny Front and camouflaged them well.

McNeill's Rangers, a Confederate partisan outfit, were one of the groups on the lookout for him. They knew that he must come out of the mountains from time to time to see his wife and children. Once they stopped one of his neighbors in a road and told him to pass on a message that he should return to his regiment. Sooner or later they'd catch up with him, they said, and when that happened they would throw him off a cliff.[9]

The exploits of the wily Potter John were numerous and have been recounted in many books and periodicals. Perhaps the most famous of these was an incident that occurred in the dead of winter. He received word through a cousin that a squad would be in the mountains on a certain day to try to snare him. He left one of his temporary shelters and walked backward for miles in the snow. His path was intercepted during the day by the provost guards, who followed to the empty hut . Since the tracks were fresh and no new snow had fallen, the men were left scratching their heads, totally baffled. The tracks led directly to the shelter and none led away from it, but their prey was not there. One of the perplexed guards remarked that Potter John must have ascended into heaven.[10]

Potter John's favorite camp, the one he felt was most secure, was in Maple Hollow, a few miles above Rawley Springs. He had some rough furniture there, a trunk for his food supply and a few books. Even though the hut was well hidden, he always approached it with caution. There were many desperate wanderers in the mountains during that last summer of the war. On one occasion, when he returned from a visit to his family, he found that his food supply had been stolen. The intruder must not have been a literary man, he decided, because the books were undisturbed.[11]

The wanted man's most unnerving encounter happened when he returned to the hollow late one night. He entered the pitch-dark hut, and was startled when something bumped violently against his leg. When he lighted the lantern, he found a large timber rattlesnake with the rear half of a rat hanging from his mouth. The rat had fixed the deadly serpent's jaws and saved Potter John's life.[12]

At the close of the war Potter John, like so many others, was finally able to return to his home and the peace that had eluded him for so long.

Charles T. O'Ferrall

Charles T. O'Ferrall grew up in Berkeley Springs, Morgan County, in what is now West Virginia. He was a Shenandoah Valley native and was a success at almost everything he put his hand to. His father was clerk of the Morgan County court, and when he died, fifteen-year-old Charles was appointed clerk *pro tempore* by circuit court judge Richard Parker of

Winchester. His appointment was supported by the members of the bar, who held him in high esteem because of his work as his late father's aide.

When he was seventeen he ran for the full six-year term and won the election with an impressive campaign. He served only two and a half years of his term, however, before Virginia seceded from the Union. Despite strong local support for the Union, O'Ferrall chose to support the commonwealth.[13]

He began his war service as a sergeant in the 11th Virginia Cavalry and at the end had risen to lieutenant colonel of the 23rd Virginia Cavalry.[14] At the beginning of the Gettysburg Campaign, in June 1863, the

Charles T. O'Ferrall, Confederate cavalry officer, U.S. congressman and governor of Virginia.

Confederate cavalry fought a series of actions with the Union cavalry in northern Virginia. The Confederate horsemen screened the army's movements beyond the mountains in the Shenandoah Valley.

As a captain in the 12th Virginia Cavalry, O'Ferrall was severely wounded in a fight at Upperville in Fauquier County on June 21, 1863. He was moved from house to house for almost a month, thus avoiding capture by federal raiding parties. Eventually he made his way to Winchester, where he suffered a relapse and "lingered on the brink of eternity." Several surgeons ministered to him and found his condition to be critical. Dr. Hunter McGuire, Stonewall Jackson's old staff surgeon, was called in and observed the wound with some surprise. The bullet had hit O'Ferrall almost directly in the center of his chest and exited near the spine. It should be noted that Charles O'Ferrall was always known for his extreme thinness. "Why, O'Ferrall," the doctor mused, "that ball ought to have hit your heart; how did it come to miss it?"

"It didn't strike my heart, Doctor," O'Ferrall replied, "because my heart was in my mouth."[15]

Following the war, O'Ferrall went to Washington College in Lexington under Robert E. Lee's presidency. He became a lawyer, a judge, a U. S. congressman and, in 1894, the governor of Virginia.

War Against Civilians

With the elevation of Ulysses S. Grant to over-all command of the Union armies in the field, the prosecution of the war took a hard turn. Grant knew that the key to winning the war wasn't capturing the enemy's capital—the key was the destruction of the southern armies and the means that allowed them to fight. This meant applying pressure on all fronts, including the supply and distribution capabilities of the Shenandoah Valley.

Before naming Philip Sheridan to command in the Valley, Grant said that he wanted to send an army there that would "eat out Virginia clear and clean as far as they go, so that crows flying over it for the balance of the season will have to carry their provender with them."[16]

General David Hunter was the first Union commander to apply the torch liberally in the Valley. Near Shepherdstown he burned homes and outbuildings alike if he thought the owners were southern sympathizers. Some of the farms thus destroyed belonged to his own distant cousins. He was observed by members of his staff to be enjoying himself.

After her house was turned to ashes, Mrs. Henrietta Lee sent Hunter a letter. It read in part, "Were it possible for human lips to raise your name heavenward, Angels would thrust the foul thing back again and demons claim their own."[17]

Hunter's actions were only a precursor of more terrible acts to be visited upon the citizens of the Shenandoah Valley. Under Sheridan, the systematic destruction of the land's bounty became the main focus of the federal program in 1864. In Rockingham County alone there were thirty houses and four hundred fifty barns burned to cinders. Anything that could be used to feed a Confederate soldier was either carried off or ruined.[18]

Battle of Piedmont

The Finley House, near the village of Piedmont, overlooks the Middle River in northeastern Augusta County. On June 5, 1864, opposing armies under Union general "Black Dave" Hunter and Confederate general W.E.

"Grumble" Jones clashed around the village, and Samuel Finley's house and other nearby structures were used as hospitals. Because it was behind the initial Union lines, the house was used as a federal surgery.

The members of the Finley family made themselves useful by assisting the doctors and their stewards in several capacities. They helped with cleaning and dressing wounds, fetched water and saw to the comfort of the men as much as the conditions would allow. Bringing solace to men who had been disoriented by the shock of battle was not an easy task. It must have been difficult for the Finleys to deal with the confusion created when their lives were slammed up against the wall of war.

Elizabeth Grattan, the Finley's married daughter, was three months pregnant at the time and had thought that her parents' farm, amid the peaceful hills and vales of Augusta, would be the safest place to await the birth of her child. Her husband, Captain Charles Grattan, was a staff officer with Lee's army in eastern Virginia.[19]

Once, as she leaned over a fallen soldier to see how he fared, he raised a bloody hand and touched her on the shoulder. The blood was fresh and left a good-sized stain on her blouse. When she felt it ooze through and saw the patch of crimson, she fainted and had to be carried from the room.

Six months later, with the scars of the battle still visible on the landscape and the house long empty of patients, Elizabeth gave birth to a daughter. The child was healthy, but those in attendance at the delivery took note of the large red birthmark on the baby's shoulder.[20]

Minnie Hedrick's Secret

Minnie Hedrick, the young girl who spoke to Stonewall Jackson in the road, had another story, one that so far as it is known, she told only once.

She was almost eight years old when the wrath of Hunter and Sheridan descended on the Valley, but it wasn't just an aggressive and destructive Union army that made the local people uneasy. When the armies weren't close, small parties of ruffians and individuals pillaged, looted and did worse on both sides of the lines.

The Hedricks had their valuables and meager foodstuffs hidden away, as did everyone in the Cross Keys area. All of the farms had been searched more than once. Most of the plunderers moved on once they found something they thought worth carrying off.

One morning when Min, her mother Eliza and a younger sister Lizzie were alone on the place, a man in blue came riding up to the gate. He forced his way into the house and demanded to know where the silver and money were hidden. Eliza told him that they didn't have any. The man went into a rage and started opening cupboards and emptying the contents of drawers out onto the floor. While he was thus occupied, the mother and girls retreated to the attic.

The soldier eventually noticed that they were missing and started to shout and curse. He went upstairs and ransacked the bedrooms and still finding nothing, became even more enraged. The incensed man called out that he knew where they were, and that he'd make them tell where their valuables had been secreted. In the next moment he started up the attic ladder, threatening what he'd do when he got his hands on them.

There *was* something hidden above, under the eaves—crocks of apple butter. When the man was half-way up the ladder, Eliza Hedrick, in terror, threw a full gallon crock down on his head. Her aim was true, and the man died almost instantly.

Eliza and little Min dragged the body downstairs and out of the house. They finally got him to a sinkhole in the orchard above the house. Eliza went back to the shed, got a shovel and buried him there. They masked the spot as well as they could, and then filled the natural depression with brush, as many people in the area did by custom.

Within a day or two other soldiers came by looking for the missing man. Eliza and her daughters were "scared to death," but convinced the men that they knew nothing about him. The secret was kept for almost ninety years.[21]

Elizabeth Heatwole

In western Rockingham County, down along Dry River, Elizabeth Heatwole struggled to keep her six children fed. One summer day the older children went on a berrying expedition and returned with an abundance of sweet, juicy berries.

Somewhere Elizabeth begged or borrowed enough flour to make a few pies from the tasty windfall. Her two eldest daughters, Nancy and Sarah, helped with the baking, while little Lizzie and her brother John rocked the baby Reuben in his cradle in a corner of the kitchen. Andrew, the eldest boy, sat at the window and daydreamed about his absent father.

The pies came out of the oven, and the aroma filled the room, almost driving the children to distraction. The pies were placed on the table to cool, and five sets of eyes bored into them in anticipation. Andrew was trying to think of the last time he had had pie when he heard muffled voices. He looked out of the window, then quickly warned his mother that two men in gray were walking up the road.

At this point in the war, foragers were indiscriminate in choosing whom to relieve of food or other goods. The color of the uniform didn't matter—friend or foe, all of the soldiers were hungry. The Heatwoles were used to thinking quickly on their feet in order to survive.

Nancy lifted baby Reuben from the cradle, and Sarah grabbed the blankets. Andrew ran over and snatched up the little feather tick. Elizabeth quickly but carefully placed the three pies in the bottom of the cradle, all in a row. The tick was placed on top of them, then the blankets, and finally baby Reuben.

The men knocked at the door, and Elizabeth opened it. Their uniforms were very ragged, but she could tell that they had been in the southern army. They asked for food, and Elizabeth told them that she had hardly enough to keep her children alive. Nevertheless, they pushed their way in and immediately picked up the scent of the fresh pies.

Where were the pies, they wanted to know. Elizabeth replied that they had just been eaten. The men searched the house anyway, but found little. The odor of fresh berry pie still filled the kitchen, and they eyed the woman and her six children with suspicion, but thinking that they had searched everywhere, they shrugged their shoulders and left.[22]

Frances Campbell

Frances Campbell volunteered her free time as a nurse at the Lutheran Church Hospital on North Main Street in Harrisonburg. In late September of 1864 she was very busy seeing to the needs of Confederates wounded in recent clashes with Sheridan's forces in the lower Shenandoah Valley. With the wounded soldiers came word that Early's army had been severely whipped at Winchester, and federal troops would almost certainly be moving southward, into the upper Valley, at any moment.

Mrs. Campbell stood on the steps of the church as thousands of federal troops passed by, heading for camps between Harrisonburg and Dayton. Suddenly her attention was riveted to a soldier carrying a knapsack that she thought she recognized. She waded into the throng and caught the man by the arm. With a shaking voice she asked him how he had come by the knapsack. His answer was something she dreaded to hear—he had taken it from the body of a dead southern officer. This was how Frances learned that her husband, Charles Campbell, a captain in the 10th Virginia Infantry, had been killed on September 19th at the third battle of Winchester.

The northern soldier told her that Charles had been buried by a whitewashed stone wall and that his name had been scrawled on it in charcoal. This information allowed her to retrieve the body later and bring it home.

Frances asked the soldier for the return of the knapsack and contents. He did not object, but asked to keep the underwear because winter would soon be coming on. She allowed him to keep the undergarments.

In the knapsack she found among a few personal items a shirt she had made for Charles. It was stained with her husband's blood, but this did not obscure where she had printed his name, company and regiment on the waist before he left for the war.[23]

Mrs. Mullins

Red Hill, now a part of the city of Harrisonburg, was once a rough district just outside of the town. A Mrs. Mullins who lived there was remembered as "the best cook you've ever seen and the best thing with the kids." She was also remembered as a rough woman who could hold her own with anyone in almost any situation. The Civil War put her nerve to the test.

Union troops occupied the environs of Harrisonburg several times during the war. On one occasion foragers looted the Mullins's smoke house and then stole the only cow the family had. When the soldiers left, Mrs. Mullins got her shotgun, loaded it, and marched off toward their camp. When she found the offenders, she confronted them, leveling the shotgun as she spoke. "You gimme my cow," she demanded, "or I'll kill every one of ya! I gotta have her to feed my children or they'll starve!"

Whether it was concern for the children or the force of her conviction to take it back anyway, they promptly obliged. It is probable that the soldiers and their friends avoided the Mullins's property for the rest of their stay in the vicinity.[24]

Rachel Houston

John and Rachel Houston lived on the fine old estate of Smithland, just north of Harrisonburg on the Valley Pike. When the war came John enlisted in the Confederate army and was away for the better part of four years.

In 1864 a large force of mostly German-speaking federal troops camped near Smithland. Some of the men looted the house and the other buildings on the place. All of Rachel's kitchen utensils and other items were "appropriated" and removed to the camp.

Several soldiers got into the attic and found some containers of soft soap that had the color and consistency of apple butter. They brought it out into the yard, got some bread, spread the soap on it and began to eat. Rachel tried to warn them that the stuff was not fit to eat, but she couldn't make them understand. The soldiers just smiled at her and said happily, "Gut, gut, lotverich, lotverich!" She finally gave up and left them to their feast.

Later, when she met an officer, she complained about the looting. The man listened sympathetically and then walked her through the camp to identify her stolen items. She was able to retrieve most of her property.[25]

A First-hand Account

Probably the best first-hand description of what happened and the bitter feelings that were aroused in the Valley in early October of 1864 was penned by a Virginia cavalryman:

> On every side, from mountain to mountain, the flames
> from all the barns, mills, grain and haystacks, and in many
> instances from dwellings too, were blazing skyward,
> leaving a smoky trail of desolation to mark the footsteps
> of the devil's inspector-general, and show a fiery record,
> that will last as long as the war is remembered, that the
> United States, under the government of Satan and
> Lincoln, sent Phil Sheridan to campaign in the Valley of
> Virginia.[26]

The Burning Bed

During the burning in the central Valley, a troop of federal cavalry swooped down on the Teel property, near Island Ford in the area of the Union approach to the battlefield of Port Republic. Only Mrs. Teel, her three daughters, her son Louis, his friend George Sipe, and the black maid were at home.

The troops fired the barn, stables and other dependencies—every building but the house was ablaze. While all of this was going on, Mrs. Teel's maid rushed into the house, screaming that she was being pursued by one of "the soldier brutes."

A soldier ran up the side porch stairway and entered one of the girls' rooms. There was a fire in the hearth, and the soldier, ignoring the pleas of the girls who stood just outside of the room on the upper side porch, grabbed a burning log from the fire and tossed it on the bed. Soon smoke poured from the window and door.

The girls were crying and wringing their hands when an officer rode by and realized what was happening. He quickly dismounted and ran up the stairs, heedless of the smoke. With his sword he impaled the burning wood and flung it out into the yard, then pitched the flaming bed ticking over the railing behind it. The house was saved.

The troops finally departed. The Teel family was in great distress as they viewed the ruins of their farm structures, but at the same time they couldn't think of words worthy enough to praise the officer who had saved their home. One of the girls, Lucy, still had tears on her face as she asserted that she would "love that Yankee" as long as she lived.[27]

Abigail Lincoln Coffman

In the vicinity of Dayton, at about the same time as the Teels suffered their ordeal to the east, many homes, barns and other outbuildings were destroyed. One house, belonging to an elderly couple, Joseph Coffman and his wife Abigail, was not consumed by flames. Several legends purport to explain why it was spared.

Some say it was left alone because it was being used as General Custer's headquarters. Others say that soldiers came to burn the dwelling but that during the preliminary looting

Abigail Lincoln Coffman

they found Mr. Coffman's Masonic apron and spared the home of a fellow Mason.

The most likely story is that Abigail Coffman, a sprightly woman, stayed their hands by declaring, "I am a first cousin of Abraham Lincoln![28] She was indeed a relative of the president. Her father, Captain Jacob Lincoln, was the brother of Abraham, President Lincoln's grandfather, who settled in Rockingham County in 1768. Abraham moved his family—including his young son Thomas, the president's father—to Kentucky in 1781.[29]

Reuben and Susanna Swope

Just to the north of the Coffman farm was the holding of Reuben and Susanna Swope. The Swopes were Brethren and took no part in the hostilities, but this didn't count for anything to the burners who arrived bent on destruction. Fires were started in all of the out-buildings, and then the soldiers turned their attentions to the house. Reuben and Susanna and the other Swope women pleaded that the house be spared, but these hard men paid no heed to the entreaties and kindled a fire in the structure. As the arsonists left, they warned the Swopes not to extinguish the fires, saying that if they returned later and found that they had done so, they would shoot them all. The family watched in horror as the flames consumed all they had built.

The fire in the house, however, was slow to catch on, and the Swopes couldn't bear to stand by idly and watch it burn. Reuben and the ladies got the slop buckets from the hog pens and threw water on the house fire. By acting quickly, they were able to put it out before it did extensive damage.

As they paused to catch their breaths, the deadly warning of the departing arsonists came back into their minds. They knew that other such threats made during the past week had been carried out.

The Swopes then did the unthinkable: they rekindled the fire and burned their own home down to the foundations.[30]

Mrs. Shank Spares Her Children

Seeing the columns of smoke rising over toward the town of Dayton, a Mrs. Shank prepared for the worse. She took her children to a remote field and made them hiding places in shocks of corn. To each she gave a loaf of bread, and she told them to stay there until she came for them.

Before long a group of burners descended on the Shank farm. The barn and other outbuildings were soon engulfed in flames, and the arsonists turned their attention to igniting the Shank home. Family members tried to remove clothes and furniture, but the soldiers threw the items back into the all-consuming flames.

The children, tucked away safely in the shocks of corn, were spared witnessing the destruction of their home. That winter they moved in with relatives who had been more fortunate than they.[31]

Mass Slaughter

Some Federals took delight in destroying the property of the people of the Valley and others somberly obeyed orders and applied the torch, but still others were obviously reluctant to burn the homes and possessions of defenseless women and children. Members of this latter group often went out of their way to inflict as little damage as possible when they could avoid it.[32]

By the end of that destructive first week in October, Sheridan began withdrawing down the Valley toward Winchester. The infantry moved slowly because of the herds of livestock they drove before them. As they passed, the federal cavalry continued to destroy barns and mills. Confederate horsemen pursued and harassed the rear elements of Sheridan's army whenever the opportunity presented itself.

About six miles north of Harrisonburg, the Federals took a large portion of the livestock—cows, hogs and sheep—to the top of a hill near Melrose Caverns and shot them. The carcasses were doused with as much combustible material as could be found, piled high with kindling dragged from nearby woodlots, and the whole mess was set ablaze. Local residents who witnessed the slaughter and conflagration said grease ran off the hill in streams.[33]

The Mills are Saved

One of the columns of Union infantry moved down the Valley Pike directly under Phil Sheridan's eye. At Edinburg, in mid-Shenandoah County, there were two large flour mills that served a wide area.

The Grandstaff mill stood hard by the pike, just south of the town.

Whissen's mill was east of the highway, beyond Stony Creek.

Several fires were started in the Grandstaff mill, but local women put them out before they could do more than scorch the timbers. Two young ladies, Nellie Koontz and Melvina Grandstaff, went to Sheridan himself and pleaded on behalf of the women and children of the surrounding countryside that the mill be spared because they depended on it for survival. To their surprise, they came away with an order protecting the structure.

Whissen's mill was defended by Confederate sharpshooters who hid in the bluffs above and beyond the mill. Every time federal torchbearers approached, they were driven off.

Eventually the northern forces moved on, and two of the district's most important mills were left intact.[34]

Aftermath

Margaret Junkin Preston of Lexington left a diary of her experiences and observations during the years of conflict. The following words from her pen probably reflect the feelings of those Shenandoah Valley residents who survived "the War":

> As after a storm has passed, we go out and look abroad to see the extent of the damage done, so now, having been swept with the besom of destruction, we look around, as soon as the calm has come, and try to collect our scattered remnants of property, and to see whether we have anything to live on.[35]

Contemporary Folktales

Folktales and legends are not confined to any one time or place and are certainly not limited to ancient history. Here are a few examples of 20th century folktales that show every sign of enduring.

The New Sidewalk

There was a woman, a formidable grande dame well into her sixties, who acted as if she considered herself to be of one class and almost everyone else to be on a much lower rung of the social ladder. She lived on the main street in the most beautiful house in Bridgewater, a large, columned, antebellum manse encircled by a white iron fence.

The street was a state route, and it was decided in Richmond in 1978 that it should be repaved and the sidewalks replaced. The old walkways were torn up, and forms were built to frame the new ones. Concrete was poured, and the surface was finished right up against the fence. The new sidewalk cured overnight, and early the next morning the work foreman, a burly man known as Big John, and his assistant, a slight man named Billy, came to inspect the job.

Big John and Billy checked the white iron gate, which was snug against the new walk, to see if it still worked smoothly. They moved it back and forth several times when "her eminence" stepped out on the portico to get her mail. She was about twenty feet from the gate.

At the moment she noticed the two men, Big John said to Billy, "It won't hitch," with some emphasis on the word hitch. The woman visibly bridled and charged off the porch. Big John's back was turned to her, but she grabbed his right shoulder with her left hand, whirled him around, and growled, "Nobody calls me that and gets away with it." He started to protest his innocence, but her right fist connected with his jaw and knocked him unconscious. Billy danced around exclaiming, "He said *hitch!* He said *hitch!*"[1]

Ghostly George

The Home Economics Cottage at Shepherd College in Shepherdstown, West Virginia, was once the home of a cobbler named George Yontz, whose companion was a black cat called Ham. George was murdered there in 1910, and no one was ever brought to justice for the crime.

Miss Net Entler moved into the dwelling and adopted Ham. Every year, on the anniversary of the cobbler's death, Ham scratched wildly at the door leading to the second floor, where awful sounds of battle emanated for about an hour on that day and then ceased abruptly. Ham then calmed down and behaved as a normal cat until the date rolled around again.

It was said that when the college purchased the property in 1917, the ghost left because he could not compete with the ruckus raised by the fraternity initiations held there.[2]

A Persistent Remedy

Some time in the second quarter of the 20th century, Dr. Edmund Tompkins of Rockbridge County was called out into the country to attend to a woman who had just given birth. The way the condition was described, he was sure that she was having "a serious post-partum hemorrhage."

When he arrived at the home, far back in the hills, he found an old woman standing over the patient with an axe. She held the sharp edge of the axe toward the suffering woman. This, the doctor was informed, would stop the flow of blood as sure as anything.[3]

Secret Not Shared

Once, while waiting in a doctor's office in Bridgewater in the early 1960s, Dr. Ellsworth Kyger ran into a woman he knew. Her family was known to have had some witch doctors in it, and Dr. Kyger asked her if she knew the form of a certain incantation. She replied that she was familiar with it, and he asked her to tell it to him. She agreed, but hesitated. Eyeing the third patient in the waiting room, Dr. Kyger's would-be informant leaned close and told him that she couldn't say it while another female was present. This goes back to the old unwritten witch doctor code that precludes secrets of magic being passed on to someone of the same sex.[4]

The Water is Wide

In the Upper Shenandoah Valley, book fairs that draw buyers from beyond the borders of the commonwealth are held several times a year. My good friend George Hansbrough of Shenandoah and I arrive early, so as to be near the head of the line when the door opens.

The Evans family, who runs the book fair, gives away thousands of old books to charities, who sell them to raise funds for their projects. There are usually two rows of give-away boxes outside, each about four boxes wide and about twenty yards long. On one particular occasion, after we had made our purchases indoors, we wandered over to these books.

As we stood there taking in the whole lot, I mentioned to George that my wife, Miriam, was an admirer of the writings of Pat Conroy of South Carolina. She had all of his books but one, and I had been searching for the obscure little volume for years without success. It was his first book, entitled *The Water is Wide,* in which he chronicles his experiences as a teacher of Gullah Negro children on one of South Carolina's sea islands.

I asked George if he thought there was a chance I might find it there that day. He admitted there was always a chance, but he looked skeptical. I glanced down at the box at our feet, which held about thirty books, and the hair on the back of my neck stood up. There it was—a near perfect first edition of *The Water is Wide!* I pointed it out to George with a shaking finger, and he took a quick step back with a scared look in his eyes.[5]

The Face in the China Press

After delivering a lecture on collecting folklore for a class at Montevideo Middle School in Rockingham County, I asked the students to share stories or experiences handed down in their families. Almost everyone had a tale to relate, and many of them were interesting and well told. The best one of the day was told by a boy with a shy and believable manner.

The young man said that not long ago his parents had brought up to the dining room an old china press that had been stored in the basement. It was dusted, and the glass panes in the doors were cleaned so that they sparkled. Within a day or so the boy noticed, out of the corner of his eye as he passed by the press, the face of an old woman. One moment the image was there, and in the next it was gone. He caught glimpses of the face frequently, and each time, for an instant, it was clear and distinct.

Eventually the boy told his mother of the apparition, and she asked him to describe the woman, which he did in as much detail as he could. His mother listened, then took him to an old trunk, from which she took out some old photographs. She sorted through them and handed one to the boy, who immediately recognized the picture as that of the old woman he had seen in the glass. His mother revealed that he was holding a photograph of his great-grandmother, and that the china press had been hers. She also told him that the old woman had died the same week as the boy was born, and that he was very much like her in many small ways.[6]

Continuing the Legacy

As long as people converse with one another with humor and irony and question things beyond their understanding, they will maintain a climate in which modern folklore can develop and flourish. The form and content of folktales will probably change by the end of the 21st century as they are influenced by new customs and technologies. They will reflect the tenor of the times in which they are born, but they will never end.

Afterword

The finest storyteller I ever knew was my great-uncle, Paul V. Heatwole (1892–1981), who came full force into my life when I was a young adult in search of an identity. Uncle Paul's fortune was his ability to remember and relate in a wonderful fashion tales of a bygone era; his gift was in never closing himself off from anyone who needed a friend.

His presence and his stories let me know who I was and let me understand why, from my earliest recollections, I had harbored twin compulsions—to create things with my hands and to lose myself in tales that took me out of the sphere of day-to-day existence. Uncle Paul introduced me to the potters, blacksmiths, silversmiths, long rifle makers, weavers and loom makers who had been my ancestors and filled my imagination with the rich stories of people who drank deep from the well of life and were moved to do memorable things.

Uncle Paul was nearly blind when I met him, yet he drew me into the stories—I *heard* the machinery of the mill grinding in the background as he described an old man having a barrel of flour hoisted onto his shoulder, and I *saw* the keen look in the sparkling, dark eyes of a gypsy queen as she told a fortune.

He died on February 26, 1981. We hadn't been sure for days whether or not he was aware of anyone's presence, but when I visited him that evening and told him how powerfully he had affected my life and how much I loved him, he squeezed my hand. He died a few minutes after I left. I was relieved that his suffering was over, but still I was crushed by the loss.

That night I dreamed I was wandering through a dark, storm-ravaged forest. The trees were bare of leaves, and they swayed wildly under rolling

Paul V. Heatwole (1892-1981) as boss of a "bark camp" (standing, hand on hip).

black and pewter clouds. The trek seemed endless, and the feeling of oppression was almost unbearable.

Finally, I came to the edge of a two-acre clearing. All was tranquil, the sun was shining, and the elements were calm. A small, white, one-room cottage sat in the middle of the grass-carpeted glade. I entered and saw Uncle Paul sitting on a white couch in front of a large window in the back wall. He smiled, patted the cushion beside him and said, "I've been waiting for you. I have a story to tell you."

At that moment I awakened and felt a tremendous burden lift from my heart and mind. Uncle Paul had let me know that he was still by my side. I hope I am an extension of him.

Notes

Valley Folk (pages 1-20)
1. WPA Writers' Program, *West Virginia*, 312.
2. Interview: William Eakle, Augusta County; and Boutwell, *Augusta County*, 35.
3. Letter from Charles Curry, *Augusta Historical Bulletin*, Vol. 6, No. 2, 27.
4. Driver, *10th Virginia Cavalry*, 143.
5. Interview: Julian Shull, Augusta County.
6. Driver, *10th Virginia Cavalry*, 143.
7. Interview: Paul V. Heatwole, Rockingham County. (Hereafter Heatwole)
8. Interview: Wade Shank, Rockingham County. (Hereafter Shank)
9. Shank.
10. Shank.
11. Shank.
12. Interview, Old Order Mennonite, Silver Lake, Rockingham County.
13. Shank.
14. Heatwole.
15. Interview: Frank Rohrer, Dry River, Rockingham County.
16. Heatwole.
17. Shank.
18. Heatwole.
19. Heatwole.
20. Heatwole.
21. Heatwole.
22. Heatwole.
23. Interview, C. Vinton Southard, Rockingham County. (Hereafter Southard)
24. Southard.
25. Heatwole.
26. Heatwole.
27. Heatwole.
28. Interview: James L. Heatwole, Warren County.
29. Huffman, unpublished manuscript; and interview: Sue Huffman Ritchie , Rockingham County.
30. Barden, *Virginia Folk Legends*, 305.

31. Interview: Dwight Shull, Bridgewater, Rockingham County.
32. Beery Family Scrapbook, Mrs. Henry Blosser obituary (*Daily News-Record*, Harrisonburg, Virginia. July 17, 1932).
33. Interview: Glenn Wine, Augusta County.
34. Interview: Nelson Alexander, Rockingham County.
35. Ritenour, unpublished manuscript, 3.
36. Interview: Roman resident, Augusta County.
37. Interview: Elmer Byrd, Rockingham County.
38. Interview: Bill Sites, Augusta County.
39. Wertz and Hutchinson, *History of the Halterman Families*, 45.
40. Interview: Nancy Garber, Harrisonburg, Virginia.

Games, Pastimes & Special Events (pages 21-38)

1. Interview: Old Order Mennonite, west of Dayton, Rockingham County (Hereafter Old Order Mennonite).
2. Interview: Maynard Hoover, Fulks Run, Rockingham County.
3. Interview: Arbutus Godfrey, Pineville, Rockingham County (Hereafter Godfrey).
4. Interviews: Mary Reid, Mt. Sidney, Augusta County; Paul V. Heatwole, Rockingham County (Hereafter Reid).
5. Interview: Wade Shank, Dry River, Rockingham County (Hereafter Shank).
6. Old Order Mennonite.
7. Interview: Ruth O. Miller.
8. Reid and Paul V. Heatwole, Dry River, Rockingham County (Hereafter Heatwole).
9. Interview: Glenn Wine, near Salem Church, Augusta County. (Hereafter Wine).
10. Wine.
11. Oliver W. Heatwole, *Sunlight and Shadow* (unpublished manuscript 1942), 5 (Hereafter *Sunlight and Shadow*); and Heatwole.
12. Interview: Margaret Landes, Roman/Seawright Spring area, Augusta County (Hereafter M. Landes).
13. Interview: Edgar Jackson Pine, Senseny Road, Clarke County.
14. Interview: Paul Landes, Roman/Seawright Spring area, Augusta County (Hereafter P. Landes); and M. Landes.
15. Old Order Mennonite.
16. Godfrey.
17. Heatwole.
18. Shank and Heatwole.
19. Interview: Lelia Swope Hertzler, Mt. Clinton, Rockingham County.
20. Shank and Heatwole.
21. Old Order Mennonite.
22. Heatwole.
23. Interview: Charles Stickley, Grottoes area, Rockingham County.
24. *Sunlight and Shadow*; Heatwole.
25. Lillie M. Ritenour (unpublished manuscript), 1.
26. Interview: Mary Sellers, McGaheysville, Rockingham County (Hereafter Sellers).
27. *Augusta Historical Bulletin, Vol. 16, Number 2*, "Christmas in Staunton, Circa 1880" (Augusta County Historical Society, 1980), 47-48.
28. Reid.
29. Interview: Nannie Jordan, Jordan's Stretch, Rockingham County (Hereafter Jordan).

30. Old Order Mennonite.
31. Interview: M. Ellsworth Kyger, Bridgewater, Rockingham County.
32. Stewart Smith and M. Ellsworth Kyger, *The Pennsylvania Germans of the Shenandoah Valley* (The Pennsylvania German Folklore Society, 1964), 113 (Hereafter *The Pennsylvania Germans*).
33. *Sunlight and Shadow.*
34. Shank.
35. Interview: Annie Lam, near Elkton on the Shenandoah River, Rockingham County.
36. Heatwole.
37. M. S. Steiner and John S. Coffman *Mennonite Evangelist* (Mennonite Book and Tract Society, Spring Grove, Pa. 1903), 20.
38. Heatwole.
39. *Sunlight and Shadow.*
40. Heatwole; F.E. Mallot, letter to Byron Berkey, Crimora, Va. 1953.
41. *Sunlight and Shadow;* Heatwole.
42. Harry M. Strickler, *A Short History of Page County, Virginia* (Dietz Press, Richmond, Virginia 1952), 45.
43. Wine.
44. Sellers.
46. Maria Koontz Carr, *My Recollections of Rocktown.*
47. Interview: Emma Byrd, Mt. Clinton, Rockingham County.
45. *Sunlight and Shadow.*
48. Interview: Frank Cline, Rushville, Bridgewater area, Rockingham County (Hereafter Cline).
49. Reid.
50. Jordan.
51. Cline.
52. Reid.
53. P. Landes.
54. Interview: Elmer Price, Massanutten Mountain, Page County.
55. *Sunlight and Shadow.*
56. Jordan.
57. Bridgewater *Herald*, March 9, 1894, "Friday Morning" (Alexander Mack Memorial Library, Bridgewater College, Bridgewater, Virginia)
58. Interview: Wade Shank.
59. Jordan.
60. Heatwole.
61. Stella Heatwole Rhodes, memoir (Hereafter Rhodes memoir).
62. Edmond Pendleton Tompkins, M. D., *Rockbridge County, Virginia* (Whittet & Shepperson, Richmond, Virginia 1952), 87-88.
63. Stan Cohen, *Historic Springs of Virginia* (Pictorial Histories Publishing Company, Charleston, West Virginia 1981).
64. *Sunlight and Shadows.*
65. Interview: John Teunis, Stribling Springs, Augusta County.
66. John W. Wayland, *A History of Rockingham County* (Reubush-Elkins Company, Dayton 1912), 438.
67. Interview: Ruby Cobb, Rockingham County.
68. Heatwole; Rhodes memoir.
69. Ibid.
70. *The Pennsylvania Germans*, 46-47.

71. Letter from Charles Curry, *Augusta Historical Bulletin Volume 6, Number 2* (Augusta County Historical Society, Fall 1969), 25-26.
72. Rhodes memoir.
73. The Bridgewater *Herald*, July 6, 1906 (G. Richard Berlin, publishers), 3.

Superstitions, Signs & a Sator (pages 39-48)

1. Interview: Old Order Mennonite, near Rushville, Rockingham County.
2. Interview: M. Ellsworth Kyger, Ph. D., Bridgewater, Rockingham County (Hereafter Kyger).
3. Stewart Smith and M. Ellsworth Kyger, *The Pennsylvania Germans of the Shenandoah Valley* (The Pennsylvania German Folklore Society, 1964), 116 (Hereafter *The Pennsylvania Germans*).
4. Interview: Daisy Halderman, North River, Augusta County.
5. Interview: Oscar Miller, Bridgewater/Spring Creek area, Rockingham County (Herafter Miller).
6. Interview: Ruth O. Miller, Rockingham County.
7. Interview: Lelia Swope Hertzler, Mt. Clinton, Rockingham County.
8. Keith Wine, "Collecting Folklore" (student paper, Bridgewater College 1977), 3 (Hereafter Collecting Folklore).
9. Interview: Paul V. Heatwole, Dry River, Rockingham County (Hereafter Heatwole).
10. Interview: Ruth O. Miller.
11. Interview: Gray Pifer, Mt. Crawford.
12. Interview: Arbutus Godfrey, Pineville, Rockingham County (Hereafter Godfrey).
13. "Collecting Folklore", 3.
14. Interview: Annie Lam, Elkton/McGaheysville area, Rockingham County (Hereafter Lam).
15. Samuel Kercheval, *A History of the Valley of Virginia* (Shenandoah Publishing Co., Strasburg, Virginia 1925), 277
16. Miller.
17. "Collecting Folklore", 3.
18. Ibid, 19.
19. Interview: Margie Roadcap Edgington, Hopkins Gap, Rockingham County (Hereafter Edgington).
20. Godfrey.
21. Keith Wine, "Collecting Folklore", 3.
22. Heatwole.
23. Godfrey .
24. "Collecting Folklore", 12.
25. Heatwole.
26. Heatwole.
27. Godfrey.
28. Lam.
29. "Collecting Folklore", 3.
30. Interview: Will Eakle, east of Mt. Sidney, Augusta County.
31. Norman Dean Jefferson, *Man in Mountainous Western Virginia, Vol. 2* (James Madison University Occasional Papers in Anthropology 6; Cattle, Sheep and Whitetail Deer), 2:100
32. "Collecting Folklore", 2.

33. Interview: Carroll Dennison, Hills of Judea, Augusta County.
34. Godfrey.
35. Heatwole.
36. "Collecting Folklore", 3.
37. Heatwole.
38. "Collecting Folklore", 2.
39. Godfrey.
40. "Collecting Folklore", 18.
41. Dana Campbell, *et al.*, *An Historic Commentary of the Jackson River Valley, Bath and Alleghany Counties, Virginia* (Occasional Papers in Anthropology No. 13, James Madison Univ. 1982), 256 (Hereafter Campbell).
42. "Collecting Folklore", 18.
43. Interview: Grace Dove, Criders area, Rockingham County.
44. Campbell, 257.
45. "Collecting Folklore", 18.
46. *The Pennsylvania Germans*, 108-109.
47. Godfrey.
48. Document: M. Otto Zigler Estate, Timberville, Rockingham County (Hereafter Zigler document).
49. Zigler document.
50. Kyger.
51. Zigler document.
52. Edgington

Remedies & Curious Cures (pages 49-66)

1. Benjamin Funk, *Life and Labors of Elder John Kline the Martyr Missionary* (Brethren Publishing House, Elgin, Ill. 1900), 38-39.
2. Interview: Glenn Wine, near Salem Church, Augusta County (Hereafter Wine).
3. Interview: Edgar Jackson Pine, Senseny Road, Clarke County (Hereafter Pine).
4. Interview: Grace Dove, Criders area, Rockingham County.
5. Printed Document purchased at a farm auction near Toms Brook, Shenandoah County.
6. Interview: Mary Z. Mason, Mayland, Rockingham County.
7. Interview: Mary Hoover, Fulks Run, Rockingham County (Hereafter Hoover).
8. Interview: Arbutus Godfrey, near Pineville, Rockingham County (Hereafter Godfrey).
9. Dr. M. Ellsworth Kyger and Patricia T. Ritchie, *Michael Baker Store Account Book, Brocks Gap, Rockingham County, Virginia 1804-1825* (Harrisonburg-Rockingham County Historical Society, Dayton, Virginia 1993) 7.
10. Interview: Gordon Barlow, Buffalo Gap, Augusta County.
11. Interview: Betty Ann Heatwole Berge, Spring Creek, Rockingham County.
12. Godfrey.
13. Interview: M. Ellsworth Kyger, Rockingham County (Hereafter Kyger).
14. Interview: Barbara Whitmore Colonna, Bridgewater, Rockingham County.
15. Interview: Eva Lee Whitmore, Augusta County.
16. Kyger.
17. Edmond Pendleton Tompkins, M.D., *Rockbridge County, Virginia* (Whittet & Shepperson, Richmond, Virginia 1952), 175.
18. Interview: James L. Heatwole, Dry River, Rockingham County.

19. Interview: James O. Swope, Rockingham County
20. Interview: Ruby Roberts Heatwole, Frederick County
21. *Pioneer America, Vol. V No.1* (The Pioneer America Society, Falls Church, VA Jan. 1973) 1-7.
22. Document: M. Otto Zigler Estate, Timberville, Rockingham County.
23. Stewart Smith, Stewart and M. Ellsworth Kyger, *The Pennsylvania Germans of the Shenandoah Valley* (The Pennsylvania German Folklore Society 1964) 131. (Hereafter *The Pennsylvania Germans*).
24. Interview: Ruth O. Miller, Harrisonburg, Rockingham County (Hereafter Miller).
25. Godfrey
26. *The Pennsylvania Germans*, 141.
27. Ibid, 161.
28. Interview: Mae Shank Blosser, Dale Enterprise, Rockingham County.
29. *The Pennsylvania Germans*, 139.
30. Interview: Paul V. Heatwole, Rockingham County (Hereafter Heatwole).
31. Interview: Eva Lee Whitmore, Sangerville, Augusta County.
32. Ona Lee Sams, Unpublished manuscript, 5.
33. Interview: Will Eakle, Augusta County.
34. Heatwole.
35. *Proceedings Vol. X* (Rockbridge County Historical Society, Lexington 1990), 166.
36. Miller.
37. Wine.
38. Pine.
39. Wine.
40. *The Pennsylvania Germans*, 130.
41. Heatwole.
42. Interview: Homer Coffman, Dry River, Rockingham County.
43. *The Pennsylvania Germans*, 130.
44. Heatwole.
45. Miller.
46. Heatwole.·
47. *The Pennsylvania Germans*, 133.
48. Ibid, 137.
49. Wine.
50. Interview: Margaret Landes, Seawright Springs/Roman area, Augusta County.
51. Hoover.
52. A. R. Harding, *Ginseng and other Medicinal Plants* (A. R. Harding, Columbus, Ohio 1908), 171.
53. Interview: Will Eakle, Augusta County.
54. *The Pennsylvania Germans*, 130.
55. *The Pennsylvania Germans*, 164.
56. John Stewart, "The Dumb Dutch of the Shenandoah Valley" (Augusta Historical Bulletin, Vol. 3 No. 1), 13. (Hereafter "Dumb Dutch")
57. *The Pennsylvania Germans*, 130.
58. *The Pennsylvania Germans*, 134.
59. *The Pennsylvania Germans*, 158.
60. "Dumb Dutch", 12.
61. Interview: Lelia Swope Hertzler, Rockingham County.
62. Will Algernon Good, *Shadowed By the Massanutten* (Commercial Press, Inc. 1992), 478.

63. Heatwole.

64. From Emanual Grove's pocket notebook, 1850-1867, Page County, original
document'

Witches & Witch Doctors (pages 67-76)

1. Peyton, J. Lewis, History of Augusta County, Virginia (second printing, C.J. Carrier
Company, Harrisonburg, Virginia 1972), 67, 166.

2. Interview: Maynard Hoover, Brocks Gap, Rockingham County (Hereafter Hoover).

3. Ritchie, Patricia T., The Family of Jacob Fawley (1802-1880) of the Brocks Gap Area,
Rockingham County, Virginia (Privately published, Winchester, Virginia 1989),
66-68 (hereafter Fawley Family).

4. Interview: Millard "Pete" Custer, Fulks Run, Rockingham County.

5. Hoover.

6. Fawley Family, 68.

7. Interview: Ruth O. Miller, Rockingham County.

8. Daily News Record, January 31, 1919 (Harrisonburg, Virginia), 3.

9. Interview: Paul V. Heatwole, Dry River, Rockingham County (Hereafter
Heatwole).

10. Smith, Stewart and Kyger, The Pennsylvania Germans of the Shenandoah Valley (The
Pennsylvania German Folklore Society, 1964), 145 (Hereafter Pennsylvania
Germans).

11. Interview: Edwin E. Root, Seawright Springs area, Augusta County.

12. Pennsylvania Germans, 145.

13. Curry Letter, Augusta Historical Bulletin, Volume 6, Number 2 (Augusta County
Historical Society, Fall 1969), 25.

14. Ibid., 23.

15. Lewis Yankey and Pat Ritchie, Brocks Gap Miscellaneous Research (Privately
published 1992), 196 (Hereafter Brocks Gap Research).

16. Interview: Eugene Souder, Rockingham County.

17. Brocks Gap Research, 196.

18. Interview: Ruby Cobb, west of Clover Hill, Rockingham County.

19. Interview: Evelyn Wine Curry, Clover Hill area, Rockingham County.

20. Brocks Gap Research, 196.

21. Interview: Margie Roadcap Edgington, Hopkins Gap, Rockingham County.

22. Evans, Robert Lee History of the Descendants of Jacob Gochenour (Carr Publishing
Company, Inc., Boyce, Virginia 1977), 92.

23. Interviews: Marie Simmers McAbee, Vada Whetzel Murphy and Arleta Clutteur,
Rockingham County.

24. Heatwole.

The Supernatural (pages 77-97)

1. Letter from Mr. Charles Curry, Augusta Historical Bulletin Vol. 6 Number 2
(Augusta   County Historical Society, Staunton, Virginia 1969), 23-25.

2. Interview: Glenn Wine, near Salem Church, Augusta County.

3. Interview: Edgar J. Pine, Senseny Road, Clarke County.

4. Published interview with Catherine Newman: Virginia Folk Legends, edited by
Thomas E. Barden (The University Press of Virginia 1991), 262 (Hereafter Virginia
Folk Legends).

5. Published interview with Harry Strickler: *Virginia Folk Legends*, 119.

6. Robert J. Driver, Jr., *52nd Virginia Infantry* (H. E. Howard, Inc., Lynchburg, Va. 1986), 47.

7. Interview: Julian Shull, Wise Hollow, Augusta County.

8. Interview: Nell Baugher, Elkton, Rockingham County.

9. Interview: Ruby Cobb,near Clover Hill, Rockingham County.

10. Interview: Mary Hoover, Fulks Run, Rockingham County.

11. Interview: Minnie Moak, Criders area, Rockingham County.

12. Interview: Maynard Hoover, Fulks Run, Rockingham County.

13. Interview: Ina Baker, Rockingham County.

14. Ibid.

15. Interview: Wade Shank, Dry River, Rockingham County.

16. Interview: Sally Joseph, Rawley Springs, Rockingham County.

17. Ralph A. Triplett *A History of Upper Back Creek Valley* (The Gregarth Company, Cullman, Alabama 1983), 105.

18. Norman Dean Jefferson *Cattle, Sheep and Whitetail Deer: man in mountainous western Virginia Vol. 2* (James Madison University Occasional Papers in Anthropology 6, Harrisonburg, Virginia), 2:98.

19. J. E. Norris, editor *History of the Lower Shenandoah Valley* (Virginia Book Company, Berryville, Virginia 1972), 388-392.

20. Joseph A. Waddell *Annals of Augusta County Virginia 1726-1871* (c. Russell Caldwell, Pub. 1901), 409-412.

21. Keith Wine, "Collecting Folklore" (student paper for M. Ellsworth Kyger's class, Bridgewater College 1977), 4.

22. Interview: Anonymous, Augusta County.

23. Interview: Paul M. Kline, near Bridgewater, Rockingham County.

24. *The Bridgewater Herald*, December 13, 1901 (G. Richard Berlin, publisher), 3.

25. Frances Huff Griffin *Wagon Road to the Western Mountains of Virginia* (McClure Printing Company, Inc., Verona, Virginia 1975), 42 (Hereafter *Wagon Road*).

26. Interview: Frances Huff Griffin, Lebanon Springs, Augusta County.

27. *Wagon Road*, 96-99.

28. WPA Writers' Program, *West Virginia, A Guide to the Mountain State* (Oxford University Press, New York 1941), 279.

29. Interview: Phillip and Pamela Ungar, Shenandoah County.

30. Interview: Margie Roadcap Edgington, Hopkins Gap, Rockingham County.

31. Ibid.

32. Wayland, John W., *A History of Rockingham County, Virginia* (Ruebush-Elkins Company, Dayton, Virginia 1912), 9.

33. Interview: Lawrence Bowers, Jr., Bridgewater, Rockingham County.

34. Interview: Linda Bowers, Bridgewater, Rockingham County.

35. Interview: Jean O'Brien, Rockingham County.

Gypsies (pages 98-102)

1. Interview: Evelyn Wine Curry, Clover Hill, Rockingham County.

2. Interview: Paul V. Heatwole, Rockingham County (Hereafter Heatwole).

3. Interview: Old Order Mennonite, Dry River, Rockingham County.

4. Interview: Evelyn Wine Curry.

5. Interview: Betty Knicely, Mossy Creek, Augusta County.

6. Heatwole.

7. Gypsy Queen obituary (*Harrisonburg Daily News-Record*, May 26, circa 1900) (Hereafter Gypsy Queen obituary).
8. Heatwole.
9. Interview: Ruby Cobb, west of Clover Hill, Rockingham County.
10. Gypsy Queen obituary.
11. G. C. (Burk) McCall death notice (*Harrisonburg Daily News-Record*, February 18, 1915).

"The War" (pages 103-119)

1. George Edgar Sipe *Civil War Recollections* (unpublished), 3 (Hereafter Sipe).
2. Interviews: Jon Ritenour (Hereafter Ritenour), Ruby Dunn Thacker and Cheryl Lyon, Rockingham County.
3. Sipe, 8.
4. Charles T. O'Ferrall, *Forty Years of Active Service* (The Neale Publishing Company, New York and Washington 1904), 140 (Hereafter O'Ferrall).
5. Interview: Paul V. Heatwole, Rockingham County (Hereafter Heatwole).
6. Samuel Horst, *Mennonites in the Confederacy* (Herald Press, Scottsdale, Pa. 1967), 125.
7. Heatwole.
8. Minnie Rhodes Carr (unpublished paper), 6.
9. Heatwole.
10. Ann L. B. Brown *Valley Mennonites in the Civil War* (Virginia Country's Civil War, Vol. 1, 1983), 80.
11. Heatwole.
12. Henry Heatwole, letter to the author April 26, 1984.
13. O'Ferrall, 81-82.
14. Robert K. Krick, *Lee's Colonels* (Morningside Bookshop, Dayton, Ohio 1979), 269.
15. O'Ferrall, 77-78.
16. Bruce Catton, *A Stillness at Appomattox* (Doubleday and Company, Inc. Garden City, New York 1953), 275.
17. Edward H. Phillips, *The Lower Shenandoah Valley in the Civil War* (H. E. Howard, Inc., Lynchburg, Va. 1993), 160.
18. D. H Zigler, *History of the Brethren in Virginia* (Brethren Publishing House, Elgin, Illinois 1914), 146.
19. Joseph H. Crute, Jr., *Confederate Staff Officers* (Derwent Books, Powhatan, Virginia 1982), 188; and Robert J. Driver, Jr., *1st Virginia Cavalry* (H. E. Howard, Inc., Lynchburg, Va. 1991), 179.
20. Interview: Bill Sites, Augusta County.
21. Ritenour.
22. Heatwole.
23. Interview: Nellie Cline, Harrisonburg.
24. Interview: Nell Baugher, Rockingham County.
25. J. Houston Harrison, *Settlers by the Long Grey Trail* (Joseph K. Ruebush Company, Dayton, Va. 1935), 485-486.
26. Frank M. Myers, *The Comanches: A History of White's Battalion, Virginia Cavalry* (Baltimore 1871), 335-336.
27. Sipe, 9-10.
28. John W. Wayland, *Virginia Valley Records* (Genealogical Publishing Co., Inc. reprint Baltimore 1965), 196.

29. John W. Wayland, *The Lincolns of Virginia* (C. J. Carrier Co. Reprint, Harrisonburg,Va. 1987), 54.
30. J. Robert Swank, *Some Records of Acker, Beery* (Singers Glen, Va. 1972), 312-313; and Swope Family History Committee, *History of the Swope Family and Descendants of Rockingham County, Virginia* (McClure Printing Company, Verona, Va. 1971), 15-16.
31. Interview: Mae Shank Blosser, Rockingham County.
32. John O. Casler, *Four Years in the Stonewall Brigade* (Morningside Bookshop reprint, Dayton, Ohio 1971), 242.
33. Interview: Thomas M. Harrison, Rockingham County.
34. John W. Wayland, *A History of Shenandoah County, Virginia* (Shenandoah Publishing House, Inc., Strasburg, Virginia 1927), 332-333.
35. Edmund Pendleton Tompkins, MD, *Rockbridge County, Virginia* (Whittet & Shepperson, Richmond, Virginia 1952), 138.

Contemporary Folk Tales (pages 120-123)

1. Interview: Bob Fred Holton, Bridgewater, Rockingham County.
2. WPA Writers' Program, West Virginia *A Guide to the Mountain State* (Oxford University Press, New York 1941), 274
3. Edmund Pendleton Tompkins, M.D., *Rockbridge County, Virginia* (Whittet & Shepperson, Richmond, Virginia 1952), 174.
4. Interview: M. Ellsworth Kyger, Rockingham County.
5. John L. Heatwole and George A. Hansbrough, Green Valley Book Fair, 1989.
6. Interview: James Everett Miles, Keezletown, Rockingham County.

Sources

Interviews

Nelson Alexander
Stephen Bagwell
Chad Baker
Ina Baker
Gordon Barlow
Nell Baugher
Betty Heatwole Berge
Mae Shank Blosser
Lawrence Bowers, Jr.
Linda Bowers
Elmer Byrd
Emma Byrd
Charles E. Cline
Nellie Cline
Arleta Clutteur
Ruby Cobb
Homer Coffman
Barbara W. Colonna
John Croushorn
Evelyn Wine Curry
Millard "Pete" Custer
Carroll Dennison
Grace Dove
Will Eakle
Margie Roadcap Edgington
Nancy Garber
Frances Huff Griffin
Arbutus Godfrey

Daisey Halderman
Thomas M. Harrison
Henry Heatwole
James L. Heatwole
Paul V. Heatwole
Ruby Roberts Heatwole
Lelia Swope Hertzler
Bob Fred Holton
Mary Hoover
Maynard Hoover
Nannie Jordan
Sally Smith Joseph
William Joseph
Paul M. Kline
Betty Knicely
M. Ellsworth Kyger
Annie Lam
Margaret Landes
Cheryl Lyon
Marie Simmers McAbee
Mary Z. Mason
James Everett Miles
Oscar Miller
Ruth Miller
Minnie Moak
Vada Whetzel Murphy
Jean O'Brien
Old Order Mennonite(4)*

Gray Pifer
Edgar J. Pine
Miriam Plecker
Elmer Price
Mary Reid
Patricia T. Ritchie
Jon Ritenour
Ruth S. Robinson
Frank Rohrer
Edwin E. Root
Matt. T. Salo
Mary Sellers
Wade Shank
Dwight Shull
Julian Shull
Warren Shull
Bill Sites
Eugene Souder
C. Vinton Southard
Charles Stickley
James O. Swope
John Teunis
Rudy Dunn Thacker
Pamela Ungar
Phillip Ungar
Effie Whetsel
Eva Lee Whitmore
Glenn Wine

*Old Order Mennonites are reluctant to be identified.

Books

Barden, Thomas E., editor, *Virginia Folk Legends* (University Press of Virginia, Charlottesville, Virginia 1991)

Boutwell, Dunlap *Augusta County, Virginia in the History of the United States*, (Kentucky State Historical Society 1918)

Campbell, Dana et al. *An Historic Commentary of the Jackson River Valley, Bath and Allegheny Counties, Virginia* (James Madison University, Harrisonburg, Virginia 1982)

Carr, Maria G. *My Recollections of Rocktown* (Good Printers, Harrisonburg, Virginia 1959)

Casler, John L. *Four Years in the Stonewall Brigade* (Morningside Books, Dayton, Ohio 1971) Reprint

Catton, Bruce *A Stillness at Appomattox* (Doubleday and Company, Inc., Garden City, New York 1953)

Cohen, Stan *Historic Springs of Virginia* (Pictorial Histories Publishing Co., Charleston, West Virginia 1981)

Crute Jr., Joseph H. *Confederate Staff Officers* (Derwent Books, Powhatan, Virginia 1982)

Driver Jr., Robert J. *52nd Virginia Infantry* (H.E. Howard, Inc., Lynchburg, Virginia 1986)

Driver Jr., Robert J. *1st Virginia Cavalry* (H.E. Howard, Inc., Lynchburg, Virginia 1991)

Driver Jr., Robert J. *10th Virginia Cavalry* (H.E. Howard, Inc., Lynchburg, Virginia 1992)

Evans, Robert Lee *History of the Descendants of Jacob Gochenour* (Carr Publishing Co., Inc., Boyce, Virginia 1977)

Funk, Benjamin *Life and Labors of Elder John Kline the Martyr Missionary* (Brethren Publishing House, Elgin, Illinois 1900)

Good, Will A. *Shadowed by the Massanutten* (Commercial Press, Inc., Broadway, Va. 1992)

Griffin, Frances Huff *Wagon Road to the Western Mountains of Virginia* (McClure Printing, Verona, Virginia 1975)

Harding, A.R., *Ginseng and Other Medicinal Plants* (A.R. Harding, Columbus, Ohio 1908)

Harrison, J. Houston *Settlers by the Long Grey Trail* (Joseph K. Ruebush Company, Dayton, Virginia 1935)

Horst, Samuel *Mennonites in the Confederacy* (Herald Press, Scottsdale, Pennsylvania 1967)

Jefferson, Norman Dean *Man in Mountainous Western Virginia Vol. 2* (James Madison University, Harrisonburg, Virginia 1982)

Kercheval, Samuel *A History of the Valley of Virginia* (C. J. Carrier Co., Harrisonburg, Virginia 1925) Reprint

Krick, Robert K. *Lee's Colonels* (Morningside Books, Dayton, Ohio 1979)

Kyger, Dr. M. Ellsworth and Ritchie, Patricia T. *Michael Baker Store Account Book, Brocks Gap, Rockingham County, Virginia 1804-1825* (Harrisonburg-Rockingham County Historical Society, Dayton, Virginia 1993)

Miller, Lula Mae *Joannes Friedrick Kirshof Genealogy* (Privately printed, Sangerville, Virginia 1981)

Myers, Frank M. *The Comanches: A History of White's Batallion, Virginia Cavalry* (Kelly, Piet & Co., Publishers, Baltimore 1871)

Norris, J. E. Editor *History of the Lower Shenandoah Valley* (Virginia Publishing Company, Berryville, Virginia 1972)

O'Ferrall, Charles T. *Forty Years of Active Service* (The Neale Publishing Company, New York and Washington 1903)

Phillips, Edward H. *The Lower Shenandoah Valley in the Civil War* (H.E. Howard, Inc., Lynchburg, Virginia 1993)

Ritchie, Patricia T. *The Family of Jacob Fawley (1802-1880) of the Brocks Gap Area, Rockingham County, Virginia* (Privately printed, Winchester, Va. 1989)

Smith, Elmer; Stewart, John; Kyger, M. Ellsworth *The Pennsylvania Germans of the Shenandoah Valley* (Penna. German Folklore Soc., Allentown, Pa. 1964)

Steiner, M. S. *John S. Coffman Mennonite Evangelist* (Spring Grove, Pennsylvania 1903)

Strickler, Harry M. *A Short History of Page County, Virginia* (Dietz Press, Richmond, Virginia 1952)

Swank, J. Robert *Some Records of Acker, Beery...* (Privately printed, Singers Glen, Virginia 1972)

Swope Family History Committee *History of the Swope Family and Descendants of Rockingham County, Virginia* (McClure Printing Co., Verona, Va. 1971)

Tompkins M.D., Edmund Pendleton *Rockbridge County, Virginia* (Whittet & Shepperson, Richmond, Virginia 1952)

Triplett, Ralph A. *A History of Upper Back Creek Valley* (Cullman, Alabama 1983)

Waddell, Joseph A. *Annals of Augusta County Virginia 1726-1871* (C.J. Carrier, Co., Harrisonburg, Virginia 1972) Reprint

Wayland, John W. *A History of Rockingham County, Virginia* (Reubush-Elkins Co., Dayton, Virginia 1912)

Wayland, John W. *A History of Shenandoah County, Virginia* (Shenandoah Publishing House, Strasburg, Virginia 1927)

Wayland, John W. *The Lincolns of Virginia* (C.J. Carrier Co., Harrisonburg, Virginia 1987) Reprint

Wayland, John W. *Virginia Valley Records* (Genealogical Publishing Company, Baltimore 1965) Reprint

Wertz, Mary Alice and Marguerite Hutchinson *History of the Halterman Families of the Shenandoah Valley, Virginia* (Privately printed 1973)

WPA Writers' Program *West Virginia: A Guide to the Mountain State* (Oxford University Press, New York, New York 1941)

Yankey, Lewis; Ritchie, Pat *Brocks Gap Miscellaneous Research* (Privately published, Rockingham County, Virginia 1992)

Ziegler, D. H. *History of the Brethren in Virginia* (Brethren Publishing House, Elgin, Illinois 1914)

Periodicals

Christmas in Staunton: circa 1880 *Augusta Historical Bulletin*, Vol. 16, No. 2, 1980
Collierstown notes: *Proceedings Vol. X*, Rockbridge County Historical Society, 1990
G. C. (Burk) McCall death notice: *Daily News-Record*, Harrisonburg, February 18, 1915
Ghost by the Road: *The Bridgewater Herald*, December 13, 1901
Glowing Toads: *The Bridgewater Herald*, July 6, 1906
Gypsy Queen Obituary: *Daily News-Record*, Harrisonburg, circa 1900
Letter from Charles Curry: *Augusta Historical Bulletin*, Vol. 6, No. 2, Fall 1969
Literary Society of Clover Hill School: *The Bridgewater Herald*, March 9, 1894
Mrs. Henry Blosser Obituary: *Daily News-Record*, Harrisonburg, July 17, 1932
Some Madstones of Virginia: *Pioneer America*, Vol. V, No. 1
Valley Mennonites in the Civil War: *Virginia Country's Civil War*, Vol. 1, 1983

Unpublished Manuscripts and Papers

Author's collection: partially printed herbal remedy, M. Otto Ziegler estate.
Author's collection: stye incantation, M. Otto Ziegler estate
Beery Family Scrapbook: obituaries
Carr, Minnie Rhodes: paper on Potter John Heatwole
David F. Heatwole collection: sator magic formula, M. Otto Ziegler estate
Heatwole, Henry: letter to the author April 26, 1984
Heatwole, Oliver W.: notes for unpublished manuscript "Sunlight and Shadow," 1942
Huffman, Leo: unpublished skating story (Augusta County)
Mallot, F. E.: letter to Byron Berkey, 1953
"Receipt for Curing Pains," Emanual Grove's Pocketbook 1850-1867, Page County
Rhodes, Stella Heatwole: memoir, Rockingham County, 1967
Ritterman, Lillie M.: unpublished manuscript
Sipe, George Edgar: "Civil War Recollections of Rockingham County"
"Universal Cure" printed document acquired at a farm sale in Toms Brook, Shenandoah County
Wine, Keith: "Collecting Folklore" (student paper, Bridgewater College 1977)

Index